Country Roads of

MICHIGAN

Drives, Day Trips, and Weekend Excursions

Third Edition

Doris Scharfenberg

COUNTRY ROADS PRESS

NTC/Contemporary Publishing Group

Library of Congress Cataloging-in-Publication Data

Scharfenberg, Doris, 1925–
    Country roads of Michigan : drives, day trips, and weekend excursions /
Doris Scharfenberg — 3rd ed.
       p.   cm. — (Country roads)
    Includes index.
    ISBN 1-56626-119-8
    1. Michigan—Tours.   2. Automobile travel—Michigan—Guidebooks.
3. Rural roads—Michigan—Guidebooks.   I. Title.
F564.3.S27   1998
917.7404'43—dc21   98-26854
                                                  CIP

Cover design and interior design by Nick Panos
Cover illustration copyright © Todd L. W. Doney
Interior illustrations copyright © Barbara Kelley

Published by Country Roads Press
A division of NTC/Contemporary Publishing Group, Inc.
4255 West Touhy Avenue, Lincolnwood (Chicago), Illinois 60646-1975 U.S.A.
Copyright © 1999, 1994 by Doris Scharfenberg
Printed in the United States of America.
International Standard Book Number: 1-56626-119-8
99 00 01 02 03 04 ML 18 17 16 15 14 13 12 11 10 9 8 7 6 5 4 3 2 1

To Leroy

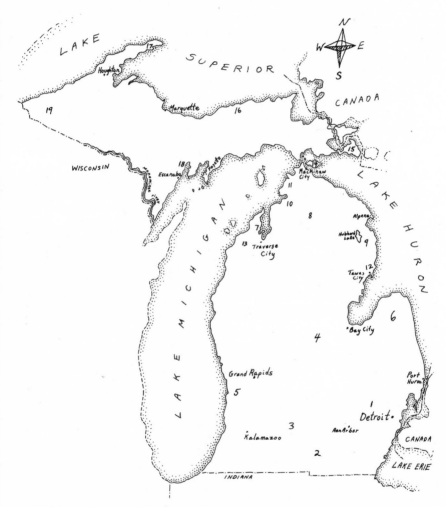

Michigan Country Roads
(Figures correspond with chapter numbers.)

Contents

Upper Peninsula

Introduction

"Let's go for a drive in the country." The suggestion has had an antique air about it, ranking with, "Let's walk to the drugstore for a soda."

Not anymore. The family jaunt down a country road for the sheer decompressing fun of it is being rediscovered. Like a mini-vacation, a rural amble is the best chance to talk as a group since the demise of the family dinner table. Call it nostalgia therapy or a stop-and-smell-the-roses experience on wheels.

Details differ slightly, but Americans share a vision of what a Midwestern country road should be like. The byway they picture is usually unpaved and winds pleasantly between rows of guardian maples and oaks, past red barns, blue silos, and trim white farmhouses. It passes small clapboard churches, remnants of one-room schools, and little sections of forest. Along this road, the next town is signaled by a water tower, the slant-roof shafts of a grain co-op, and the narrow spire of a church steeple.

In this vision, people drive tractors, auction antiques, serve coffee, or sit on wide front porches. Deserted farms with sagging barns and old wagons rusting in the front yard are thought of as picturesque.

Right off a Norman Rockwell or *Farm Journal* calendar, this dream road has plenty of Michigan editions—even when traffic on the interstate can be seen across someone's back forty or when the next town on the map is announced by high-rise gas and fast-food signs.

Michigan, however, is not the Midwest norm. It is a peninsula, surrounded on three sides by the largest reservoir of fresh water on earth. If the 3,117-mile coast were twisted into a rope it would stretch from New York to San Francisco and dangle in both oceans. With over 10,000 inland lakes and this wondrous coast, water dominates our "countryside" as much as land. Nearly all state roads skim lakes or lead eventually to the wide horizons of Michigan's boundaries.

Another fact of Michigan life (shared with Wisconsin and Minnesota) is the botanical change from south to north—from predominantly farmland with a sprinkling of forests to endless square miles of forest with a sprinkling of farms. Although the state's famed fruit belt goes straight up its western coast, anyone driving north on I-75 from Detroit should notice the change in the vegetation patterns is dramatically swift.

You'll need a road map. These excursions are designed for a day or a weekend. But Michigan is a big state; it may take you a day just to get to the start of some of these country roads. Whether you're starting from Detroit, Toledo, Gary, Chicago, or Toronto, you'll find places to visit that you've never heard of before.

There is no way to exhaust Michigan country road possibilities. Ambling through forested stretches of Newago, Lake, Mecosta, Oceola, Wexford, and other western counties, there are rural restaurants, canoe rivers, good fishing lakes, bike trails, cross-country ski trails, hobby shops, little hamlets with hot cider or muffins ready. Going up the center of the state on old U.S. 27 will take you to the tall-timber beauties of the Hartwick Pines, to off-path little motels where friendly hosts are twice as glad to see you, to places where people take their time . . . and know where the points of interest are. The State Travel Bureau (P.O. Box 30226, Lansing, Michigan 48909, or call 800-5432-YES) has material on fall tours, farms, B&Bs, charter boats, golf, antiques, special events, and much more.

Take a country road, any country road, and re-create yourself.

1

Three Country Outings

(on Roads Near Detroit)

Getting there: Take an Oakland County refresher or go west via North Territorial Road or meander south.

Highlights: Meadow Brook Hall, antiques, the Holly Hotel, Matthaei Botanical Gardens, lakes, U-pick farms, old mansions, Westcroft Gardens, Hathaway House, and Keeney Orchards.

These short excursions designed for fall color, spring breaks, and winter wanderings are close to the Detroit metro area, yet one thousand sensory miles from megabig pressures. Directions are as precise as possible, but don't leave home (wherever you start from) without your basic piece of equipment, a road map. Remember that the top of the map is north, the right side east, etc. (If you are astonished that some people may not know these truths, just ask AAA agents who specialize in routes for directionally dysfunctional drivers.)

An Oakland Country Refresher

Exit I-75 north at Pontiac Road to go east (or take Adams Road north) and head around to the east end of the Oakland

University property, following signs to Meadow Brook Hall, a
Tudor home beyond all dreams.

Elegant, rich, poetic, and low-key enough to be inviting,
the mansion is the dream of Matilda Dodge Wilson, daughter
of Canadian German immigrants, saloon keepers in a Detroit
long gone. Matilda's charms won the heart of automaker John
Dodge, who died and left her multimillions. With her wealthy
second husband, Alfred Wilson, she embarked on a long-trea-
sured house-building plan, and the results are now a part of
Oakland University's heritage.

Money was clearly no problem for the Wilsons, who filled
their home with art and comforts—from a magnificent organ
in its own room to a bedroom for Matilda fit for Marie
Antoinette.

Public tours are limited to Sunday afternoons (1 to 4 P.M.)
although there are guided tours in July and August. (Ask about
early December tours.)

If you can't get in, at least walk around. A simple rose garden and huge spread of lawn are lovely in themselves, but the
house with its many chimneys, mullioned windows, and warm
tones (especially against the bright yellows and reds of fall
trees) will devour your heart and your film. It is a measure of
Matilda's spirit that she donated the whole place with many
furnishings intact, plus extra land and money, to help fund the
university.

When you can tear yourself away, turn north on Adams
Road, right on Tienken Road, left on Washington Road, and
right on 26 Mile Road. It sounds complicated but isn't, as you
are merely angling your way over to the entrance of the Stoney
Creek Metropark, sprawling acres on meandering road
through hickories and oaks, past picnic areas, hike-bike trails,
and the joys of a sizable lake. There's a visitors center and a
nature center with a great bird-watcher's window. A park
sticker is required and worth every penny.

Backtrack to Tienken Road, turning right (north) on Orion Road, on up to lunch and antique shopping in Lake Orion, another little town threatened by popularity.

On Indianwood Road from Lake Orion west to Dartmouth, north to Stanton. . . . The idea is to go north a mile or so, then west on whatever takes your fancy. It's difficult to get too lost as long as you keep turning west and north, and these backcountry roads are full of nice surprises like little vegetable stands, lawn sales, or front-porch antique dealers. You'll pass M-26, Lapeer Road. If you wind up in Lapeer, "Gateway to the Thumb," consider that a bonus. Lapeer is a delightful place with a historic courthouse presiding over midtown. Cross M-15 (to Ortonville) and I-75; signs will indicate the way to the Holly Recreation Area, another retreat for bird watching, hiking, fishing, and cross-country skiing in the winter. You'll pass nice hills with wide scenic vistas and fields filled with a botanist's list of wildflowers. Winter downhill skiing is nearby.

Country roads, farms, and the winsome town of Holly preside over the northwest corner of Oakland County. Although Holly's north side has the modern endearments of fast food and discount shops, more than 40 places in Holly are on the National Historic Register; that should clue you in. Holly's lively past is alive and well. Wander south downtown, past antique shops and Battle Alley, where Carrie Nation shattered saloon glassware with her wide-swinging umbrella. (No ax this time.)

All doubts will vanish over a meal at the Holly Hotel, restored to its Victorian ambience right up to the bar, quaintly labeled with a genuine sign that reads DISPENSING DEPARTMENT.

From Holly, Millford Road south to a left turn at Ranch Road takes you to a final windup at Diehl's Orchard and Cider Mill. Apples are the star of their show, but pears, plums, fruit jams and jellies of all kinds are there with doughnuts, popcorn, picnic tables, and cider in all its tangy glory. Open all year, Diehl's makes a good winter stop before heading down the pike to home.

For More Information

Meadow Brook Hall, 248-370-3140

Stoney Creek Metropark, 800-24-PARKS

Holly Recreation Area and Visitors Information, 248-634-1900

Holly Township Office, 248-634-9331

Holly Hotel, 248-634-5208

Diehl's Orchard and Cider Mill, 248-634-8981

West via North Territorial Road

Close to M-14 and M-23, just east of Ann Arbor, the Matthaei Botanical Gardens (on a country road called Dixboro between Plymouth and Geddes Roads) will have you thinking in terms of potting and planting even as winter is landing its first blows.

A University of Michigan research facility, Matthaei thrives on variety. Outside on the 300-acre site or inside the high glass roof of the conservatory, there are carefully controlled environments and specialized clusters. You'll see ferns or cactii, medicinal herbs or purely ornamental blooms, and special little touches like the goldfish pond.

Park the car and walk (no roads through here) on a self-guided tour to get a whiff of the tropics or desert or wander the four outdoor trails along a little stream. You'll find 750 kinds of grasses, flowers, shrubs, and trees, plus grow-your-own or identification books and seeds in a little gift shop.

Go north on Dixboro to North Territorial Road, one of the state's true historic pathways. Head west, exactly as so many early settlers did when the Territory of Michigan was opening up to eastern and European newcomers. The road is pure country, skimming past farmhouses of plain cube or slightly L-shaped design—no fancy Queen Anne porches decked with gingerbread trim. You'll pass a small cemetery and a converted but recognizable one-room school.

Be creative in your wandering. For example, driving south on Whitmore Lake Road to Northfield Church Road and turning west, I found the corner church a red brick structure of unusual appeal. The church and yard looked to be out of a bucolic poem. The denomination didn't matter to me; I am determined to attend service there some summer's day. A right turn at Jennings and it's back to North Territorial Road.

After tunnels of oaks and gentle vistas of plowed acres, commerce is confined to the hamlet of Hudson Mills, just beyond the entrance to Hudson Mills Metropark, another tempting detour. You'll find lengthy hiking paths along the Huron River, picnic tables, and seldom any crowds. In the full flash of fall color, these splendid Metroparks that circle southeast Michigan should be destinations, not just a passing impulse.

The Pinckney and Waterloo Recreation Areas spread their patchwork acreage just beyond the junction of North Territorial Road and M-52. (There are a lot of private land parcels amid the public system, so be careful not to trespass.) Dozens of lakes glisten behind the woodlands. Besides the obvious signs, you can often tell a U-pick farm by the loaded trucks with a tailgate display arrangement in the driveway. Go fish, pluck fruit, and keep moving.

Turn south on M-52 to Chelsea, home of Jiffy mixes, and the Common Grill, a good place for lunch. The restaurant went through some heavy remodeling to appear as it does today, but high tin ceilings, hardwood floors, and murals of old Chelsea rooftops make it an interesting sip-and-stare experience.

Turn toward Ann Arbor on Jackson Road, following it right into the heart of this famed university center, past Main to Fifth and then north (left two blocks). This brings you to a "country place," the farmers' market. You may arrive at the wrong time of day or week, but make a note of this location and plan to return at the correct time to buy unusual veggies and herbs, all genuine bargains.

The area is a warren of cut-rate shops (a resale place called the Treasure Mart is extremely popular), and a snack stop at Zingerman's Delicatessen (corner of Detroit Street and Kingsley) is required eating. Many think this is the best deli in the state, and all the states around it, offering 40 sandwich choices, slab-size wedges of cheese, and German and Jewish breads and bagels.

There's more country road ahead if you follow Pontiac Trail north and then take a right at one of the mile roads, Seven or Nine, for example.

For More Information

Matthaei Botanical Gardens, 734-998-7060

Hudson Mills Metropark, 1-800-24-PARKS

Common Grill, 734-475-0470

Zingerman's Delicatessen, 734-663-3354

A Sweet Meander South

In Detroit, take Jefferson (or Southfield to Jefferson) to Wyandotte, where the street name turns to Biddle, and on to Riverview and Trenton—not exactly a country road, but with certain gentle joys.

In Wyandotte are two marvelous old mansions facing each other on Biddle Street like a pair of dowager queens. Once showplace Victorian homes, the one on the "river" side is now a public library, the other is the Wyandotte Historical Museum. See how grandma may have lived if she were rich—carved oak, stained glass, the plush look of opulence. Trimmed for Christmas, the museum becomes a living greeting card and a perfect backdrop for brides who like to rent the place on weekends for "homey" weddings.

Farther along there are two bridges to Grosse Isle: one is a toll (from Riverview), and one is free (from Trenton). A drive along this 12-mile-long and affluent retreat on the lower end of the Detroit River barely hints at its history of farms and woodlands. In 1860 wealthy Detroiters began building summer homes on the riverbank where they could watch the boats passing from their gazebos and wide front lawns. As the 19th century steamed downstream and two world wars unfolded, the farms diminished and woodlands thinned. Grosse Isle became its own tight little enclave with a private school system and post office. For a while there was a U.S. Naval Air Station at the south end.

As you circle the shore you won't find parking places for visitors to stop and enjoy the view, but there are no rules against gazing at the old cottages with their Gothic or Queen Anne splendor still intact. Grosse Isle supports a small shopping area and a restaurant or two.

Learn more about residents like Ransom Olds, Oldsmobile founder, at the East Side Station, the Grosse Isle Historical

Museum. The hours are Thursday 9:30 AM to noon and Sunday 1 PM to 4 PM. No phone. There are island brochures and maps available sometimes. Ask.

One more stop should be the Westcroft Gardens at 21803 West River Road, south of Church Road. Rhododendrons and special northern varieties of azaleas abound in mid-spring. You'll find ground covers, wildflowers, annuals, and herbs plus 12 acres of greenhouses. A nursery for all seasons, but call for hours.

Down Jefferson again, the Lake Erie Metropark Entrance lies between Meyers Road and Huron River Drive. I'd skip the wave pool, ski center, first-aid and food loop to the left (unless you have a small fry to placate) and enjoy the subdued pleasures of keeping to the right for huge arching trees, wide grassy lawns, and a view of Lake Erie.

Take Jefferson on to Sigler Road, turn right to M-24 (Telegraph Road), and south to Monroe, the town noted for General George Custer, La-Z-Boy chairs, great pageants, and muskrat dinners—an old Indian-settler tradition still practiced on annual occasions by local lodge groups. A town for old-house addicts, Monroe was founded by the French and was once a hot contender for the metro role that went to Detroit. Time should be spent walking around Loranger Square at the corner of First and Washington. You'll see a vintage courthouse, a house turned into a library, and the site of a whipping post (rare in the Midwest—there's no record that it was ever used).

Custer's reputation has dimmed in recent times, but at the very interesting Historical Museum (filling up a former post office, 126 South Monroe) you can buy a poster that reads:

I WANT YOU
FOR THE US CAVALRY

Join me and the illustrious 7th.
Help put down the militant Sioux.
(signed) George A. Custer

Time to hit a country road again.

Take M-50 west from Monroe Street to Lewis Avenue, south/left to Ida Center Road, Blissfield Road south into town. The fields that line these lanes are of rich soil; they were sold for a little over a dollar an acre when Michigan became a state.

Maybe you spotted its picture on a billboard, but even without advertising Hathaway House in Blissfield is destined for a modest measure of fame. A grand Greek Revival house that was turned into an all-American restaurant, it feels as comfortable as a favorite aunt's back porch, but classier. Six dining rooms serve excellent food, with desserts that put you on cloud nine. On Sunday the smorgasbord, where sweet hot breads, six-layer cakes, and Jamaican coffees will totally bust any diet, should have its own fan club. (Try the chocolate peanut-butter pie to see what I mean.)

There are some interesting specialty shops on Blissfield's Adrian Street (U.S. 223) where the Hiram Ellis Inn just might have one of its four rooms available.

West to Adrian, seat of Lenawee County with an appropriately ornate Romanesque county courthouse, is an extra-pleasant college town and once a main stop on a Toledo–Chicago rail run.

Turn north on Tipton Road, then west at Tipton for two treats. One is at Keeney Orchards for apples or sweet and tart cherries, July through mid-September, and the other is Michigan State University's Hidden Lake Gardens, a landscape arboretum open to the public and described in Chapter 2.

Zigzag back to Detroit if you don't want to take U.S. 12

home or go back on M-50 Britton and Ridge Road, which goes up to Ypsilanti, Michigan Avenue, and points east.

For More Information

Westcroft Gardens, 734-676-2444

Hathaway House, 517-486-2141

Hiram Ellis Inn, 517-486-3155

2

The Chicago Road

(U.S. 12)

Getting there: From Detroit (east to west), take I-94 west about 40 miles, then turn south on M-23 and exit at U.S. 12, the first exit. U.S. 12 runs about 160 miles across the state, to Indiana and the Chicago suburbs.

Getting there: From Gary or Chicago (west to east), take I-94 northeast and join U.S. 12 just across the Michigan state line in New Buffalo.

Highlights: Don't miss the antique shops and sleepy town charm in Saline, Clinton, Allen, and Niles, the rolling farm country, the Irish Hills, twin towers, Hidden Lake Gardens, Ed Drier's butcher shop at Three Oaks, the Warren Dunes, wineries, and pick-your-own fruit.

I n its swift minute of history against the mists of Indian time, Michigan owes much to those who knew the territory first. Our highways are among the debts.

Until 1812, Sauk Indian tribesmen of the Illini wore a narrow footpath between the big waters of Lake Michigan and the regions around Lake Erie. Winding through forests, curling around lakes, the Sauk Trail was nonetheless quite direct.

Incoming Europeans followed its sure guidance to reach settlements or to journey to Chicago.

Foot trails widened to dirt roads, the Sauk Trail evolved into the Chicago Pike, and then into U.S. 12. Clusters of cabins grew up to be Saline, Coldwater, Niles . . . and the changes of 200 years are chronicled along the highway that went from main route to fast-lane orphan. I-94's concrete conveyor belt left the old road looking lost for a while, but for those not trying to cross the state before the next news broadcast, U.S. 12 (still known as "the Pike") restores a human pace.

Easygoing, active, scenic, and historic. During the fresh bursts of spring, or in fall when sugar maples and birches are in full autumn color, red barns and green lawns are straight from a child's coloring book. Lakes glisten through the trees (in Michigan you are never more than six miles from a body of water); hills are gentle, rolling, and seductive.

U.S. 12's east end is Michigan Avenue in Detroit. It acts as Main Street for Dearborn and the university city of Ypsilanti, angling south and west. When the highway crosses M-23, a north-south expressway, the roll of country road (depending on how "citified" your thinking is) begins. Farm-equipment sales replace car lots; there are more antique shops and less traffic. Most communities are the right size for a healthy pedestrian to amble through before lunch.

Just west of M-23, a beautiful old Empire-style home on a large corner lot sets the mood for Saline, home to one of the largest antique dealers in the state. For the next 150 miles "ye olde" shops seem as plentiful as farm silos.

If anyone is searching for a particularly hard-to-find item (engraved ivory toothpicks), they reach for the *Saline Reporter*. Its sales boxes have no locking mechanism; you are trusted to put the money in the canister before grabbing the paper. Those accustomed to the clenched-fist devices of the wider world are apt to find this as quaint as button shoes.

On the west edge of town the barn-red Weller's mill is a landmark. No mill any more, though, just antiques and a cozy restaurant. The original gristmill was about to fall board by board into the passing Raisin River when Henry Ford spotted it in the 1920s and redid the structure for use as a soybean oil processing plant. On the walls of the café, next to pipes left from soy days, photos show various stages of the restoration.

Mr. Ford (no one called him Henry) covered all bases. He found a schoolhouse and had it moved to a site across from the mill so his employees' children could go to school right there. The school is now a private home, complete (I was told) with one of the original blackboards.

Westbound again, U.S. 12 (now with bike-path shoulders) curves in wide arcs instead of the tight twists of its first paved years. I wondered why so many barns were on one side of the road while farmhouses were on the other and came up with my own theory: Speeds over 30 mph require a straighter bead on the horizon, so a force called eminent domain hit farms broadside. "They're putting that dern road right between us and the chicks!" There was a hazard to face every time the cows needed milking.

However, for city kids, whizzing close to pigpens and watching tractors without leaving the car was a form of visual education. Many a Detroit child was introduced to cows and sheep on roads like U.S. 12, myself included. Southern Michigan is also big in sheep and horse raising.

More antique shops cluster in Clinton, next town west, where yesterday's china teacups pour out little pots of money. Like Saline (and all the towns on the Pike), Clinton lends itself to sidewalk strolling. Giant trees, inviting front porches, low noise levels.

The largest antique in town is the Clinton Inn, a vintage charmer on the main intersection restored to host-house condition with tender care. Three stories tall, the inn opened as a hotel in 1901 with a ballroom over the store next door and a drummer's room where traveling salesmen could spread out their wares to—of course—drum up business. That space is now the tavern. A golden oak staircase gleams, lace curtains are fresh, the clock tower's timepiece really works, and floors do just the right amount of creaking. Makes you want to step down the block and shop for spats, button hooks, and maybe a horsehair settee for the parlor. In Clinton you'd find them all.

Personally, I love detours, especially those that cut through places I can't get to otherwise. The nonprofit Southern Michigan Railroad operates 45-minute trips to Tecumseh on summer weekends. Closed coaches or open gondolas, a nostalgic bumping through woods and wetlands, and on to shopping in Tecumseh. The depot/museum is on Division Street, nothing too fancy; just south of U.S. 12.

The last shred of an old-style gas station sits forlornly in tall grass west of town. The roof that overhung the gas pump (gone) is badly a-tilt. No more connection to the road; a melancholy metaphor for life. I am hoping that the Wyeth-looking structure is enjoying a second life as a photographic art object. Immortality on a gallery wall is not all bad.

Another turn or two and our road passes Bauer Manor (fine restaurant) on Evans Lake at the edge of the Irish Hills. White columns give a Southern-belle look to the two-story white frame Michigan historic site (its story on a memorial plaque) where the last stagecoach stopped for hot soup and biscuits in 1900. It's been a post office, general store, you-name-it, and is one of the oldest continuously operating businesses in the state.

The low contours of the emerald hills, a geographic gift touching several southeastern Michigan counties, were a leprechaun's call to Dublinesque immigrants. Lakes like embedded mirrors reflect the Aulde Sod's 30 shades of green, and Monaghans, Kelleys, and Brightons still dominate the phone book 150 years after the first potato famine refugee arrived.

The Irish Hills have long been working-class Poconos to many Detroiters—affordable escape country. In Dearborn's Henry Ford Museum adjacent to Greenfield Village, a display depicting the impact of autos on American life includes one of the first tourist cabins ever built. Curators found this primitive gem in the Hills.

Some fairly imaginative stagecoach enterprises ("fab fun for the whole family") have come and gone through the years. (Stagecoach Stop, USA, is one of the best.) The good part is that this short stretch in the heart of the Hills has not gone out of control. Amusements are clean, well-run, and not too outrageously priced, and the peaceful presence of Hayes State Park offers space when your pint-sized Olympians need to run around.

A familiar sight to Hills goers are twin towers that look like giant salt shakers and stand about as close to the highway as they can get. Two seems a tad overdone. It started when a fellow named Kelley once owned half of the hill; the Michigan Observation Company (MOC) owned the other half. The MOC planned a sightseeing tower, an idea that incensed Kelley, who chose to leave his pristine hilltop alone.

The MOC built one anyway (1924), smack against Kelley's lot line—which so roused Kelley's considerable Irish dander that he built a higher tower, hoping to block part of their view. The MOC went higher. Kelley went higher. The MOC planned a super-high steel tower, a final blow to Kelley's wallet. Kelley quit. Both parties are long gone, and the towers have had one owner for many years. For 50 cents and a hearty climb, you get a great panorama.

Very close to the towers, the Shrine of St. Joseph on the shore of Wamplers Lake draws Catholic pilgrims and those interested in folk art. During the Depression an unemployed Italian tile setter made colored tile and cement Stations of the Cross. I thought they were just corny when I attended college near here, but I have learned to see through a wider lens.

Another detour. Southeast of Cambridge Junction on M-50 about 10 miles are Hidden Lake Gardens, Michigan State University's landscape arboretum. Breathe deeply. Hanging baskets of exotic blooms, as well as desert and jungle plants, thrive under glass domes. Wild lilies edge the woods and labeled canopies of birch, oak, and maple arch over the road. Ice stops the outdoor show, but indoors it's always spring.

Back at the junction the brick building on the south side says Walker Tavern Antiques; sitting pretty on U.S. 12's north side is Walker Tavern State Historical Park. Once guests stayed in the tavern for a quarter but took chances on getting a bunk-mate fresh from three days on a horse.

Somerset, Moscow, Jonesville, Allen, Quincy; not a strip mall or K-Mart in sight. Now and then an Amish buggy or a week-end farm auction.

And barns. Workhouse, warehouse, nursery, refuge, health indicator of a farm; the silent watchers on a country road. From bright red and prosperous to time-beaten relics with traces of Mail Pouch tobacco ads still visible, soaring agri-cathedrals or humble helpers, this is high-per-capita barn land. Watch a farmer's eyes when he's talking about his barn. Like a captain's ship or a trucker's rig, a good barn evokes pride and affection. No two-car garage will ever excite someone who has lived and worked in a lofty old barn.

If you expound like that in Jonesville, they may think you're daft. A barn is just a barn, they'll note, but take that house of Elijah Myers. . . . Myers, the architect who designed Michigan's gloriously Victorian state capitol, built a house in Jonesville for a rich banker. Three blocks south of U.S. 12 on Maumee, the Grosvenor House Museum is steeped in opulence and drama. You expect characters from an Ibsen play to walk through. Jonesville history is documented upstairs.

Allen, the "Antique Capital of Michigan," has nearly 90 dealers who operate under signs proclaiming "Simple Treasures," "Poor Richard's," or the "Quilt Lady" where handmade Amish coverlets are decently priced. Green Top Village (a resettlement of "orphan" buildings) and Country Mall give everyone plenty to paw through.

Mall-motel-and-big-Mac (i.e., the 1990s) returns on the fringes of Coldwater, approximately midway on the Detroit-Chicago run. In the heart of this working-class town lies a warm Coldwater that supports summer theater and likes to point out the houses on Chicago Street (U.S. 12). The Empire-style Wing House Museum is one of those rare places with original furniture including the personal contents of drawers.

One house, built by a banker in 1903 for $15,000, is facing the future as a spectacular bed-and-breakfast. The style is Colonial Reform (like the White House), and parquet floors, roses on the wallpaper, and antique coverlets make you forget time. Breakfast settings are fit for a duchess.

The road angles down toward the Indiana state line, through Sturgis (more fast food, one Holiday Inn) and White Pigeon, through more farmland and recreational areas.

Niles, the big city of the trip (population 13,000), requires a business route detour. Straddling the St. Joseph River, the Niles locale has been under four flags (British, French, Spanish, and American), a theme for the brochures.

Steering wheels, air bags, and Simplicity Patterns keep Niles working; an elegant city hall keeps it running. Few

towns do business in a Queen Anne mansion. Visitors saun-
tering into this Victorian castle during the workday see the
elaborate hall fireplace or gaze up the wide stairwell where
light from stained glass casts a warm glow on everything.

Banker Henry Chapin completed his fine house in 1884,
and it was bought by the city at auction in 1932 for $300. The
price was so right because Chapin's grandchildren stipulated
that it could only be used for civic purposes and never altered
or remodeled in any way—not even to move the door with a
large and beautiful multicolored glass panel that opens only on
a small dark closet. No light shines through to bring out the
glory of the glass; too bad.

The Chapin carriage house has been transformed into the
Fort St. Joseph Museum containing (quoth the Smithsonian)
one of the best collections of Plains Indian artwork in the
United States. Al Capone slept in Niles (uneasily, we hope) at
the Four Flags Hotel, the classiest guest house in southwestern
Michigan when it opened in 1925 at the corner of Fourth and
Main. The hotel has also hosted Eleanor Roosevelt, Knute
Rockne, and Truman Capote. They probably arrived by train,
stepping into a neo-Romanesque station recently discovered
by Hollywood for swift flashes in *Continental Divide*,
Midnight Run, and *Only the Lonely*.

In the midst of a fall 1848 thunderstorm, Niles's first train
arrived to a brass band, artillery salvos, and bonfires; bringing
the railroad to Niles was clearly a welcome moment. A depot
was built but destroyed by fire. A second depot nearly rotted
away. It took the announcement of the 1893 Columbian
Exposition in Chicago and the chance to impress everyone
who would be passing through Niles to see the show for town
founders to build the present station. A real coup for Niles.

The new red stone showpiece had a clock tower, a terra
cotta fireplace, carved oak paneling, fresh muslin curtains, all
of it. There was even a greenhouse for extensive gardens. But

those times passed. By the 1970s the station was a sooty endangered specimen until Amtrak and the Michigan Transportation Department funded a restoration. They saved a jewel.

Buchanan, hardly five minutes from Niles, has a gristmill doing what gristmills are supposed to do, and you can purchase the flour. Pears Mills is a restoration, of course, and one of the best, although the handicap of being in a midtown parking lot detracts some from the charm.

A nature-loving teacher and her husband from Chicago bought a piece of property on the St. Joseph River between Buchanan and Berrien Springs that will mesmerize any detouring gardener. Arranged like small rooms, gardens of different purpose float down the hillside and into personal niches. There's ferns, boxwood, heather, lilies, wild asters, and a visitors center restaurant where you sip herbal tea and bite into health foods. It's called Fernwood.

Back to U.S. 12 and Three Oaks, where a couple of items so low-key as to be barely audible turn out to be rather fascinating. One is a butcher who stuffs sausages and smokes hams with old German know-how. Ed Drier's little butcher shop has sawdust on the floor, old butcher tools on nearby hooks, and is so tuned to times past that his domain has been proclaimed a National Historic Site.

No refrigerated bin with prepackaged helpings here. Tell Ed your choice and the slicing begins. Bill Mauldin, Ivan Albrecht, Larry Hagman (J. R. Ewing), and, of course, professional wanderer Charles Kuralt have been here. Press clippings, platters, tiles, and even a dapper pig in a necktie line the walls while a carousel cow stands in the window near a sign saying BARE FEET ACCOMPANIED BY MONEY MOST WELCOME.

I walked out with more sausage than I eat in a year.

The other item (trivia you'll never find on *Jeopardy!*) lies in the shell of an old factory with the words "Warren Featherbone Company" still visible on the side. In the mid-1800s, when fashion dictated hoop skirts as well as the tonnage of heavy fabric and heavier whalebone, E. K. Warren ground up some turkey feathers, reshaped them with his own glue, and voilà—lightweight hoops. They sold like crazy. Every lady from the shady ones in Silver City to Queen Victoria's court wore featherbone hoops under her skirts. Here in Three Oaks was one of the most successful businesses in the world.

Warren's wealth was used wisely. He bought land along Lake Michigan just to preserve it; Warren Dunes State Park, minutes from where U.S. 12 curves south toward Chicago, is part of that purchase.

More info, maps, chitchat, and even bikes to rent are available in the Three Oaks Bicycle Museum, a font of local data.

The western end of U.S. 12 is a beeline through fruit country; it's U-pick heaven and the livin' is juicy. In spring Berrien County side roads are excursions into living postcards as blossoming trees billow where snow has just melted and vineyards come back to life. In fall these back lanes lead the color tour list.

In prime Michigan wine territory, mavens watch for signs to tasting rooms (Lemon Creek Fruit Farms and Tabor Hill; more up in Paw Paw) or pick their own grapes, peaches, strawberries, or blueberries to make home wine or just eat till their chins drip.

U.S. 12 crosses its speedier cousin, I-94, at New Buffalo on Lake Michigan. Quiet New Buffalo is flexing new summer muscles with waterfront condos and bigger marinas. The old roundhouse may survive as a mini-mall; its depot on the Chicago-Detroit run has been turned into a small rail museum with a mannequin trainman rechecking his schedule, but interest here has turned from farms and barns and inland crossroads to boats and lighthouses and channels with long ships passing. The Indiana state line lies minutes away.

For More Information

Clinton Inn, 517-456-4151

Southern Michigan Railroad Society, 517-456-7677

Bauer Manor, 517-431-2506

Stagecoach Stop, USA, 517-467-2300

Golden Nugget Steak House, 517-467-2190

Irish Hills Trading Post, 517-467-2775

Hidden Lake Gardens, 517-431-2060

Grosvenor House Museum, 517-849-9596

Allen Antiques Mall, 517-869-2492 (dealer)

Wing House Museum, 517-278-2871

Chicago Pike Inn, 517-279-8744

Fort St. Joseph Museum, 616-683-4702

Fernwood Nature Center, 616-695-6491

Drier's Butcher Shop, 616-756-3101

Three Oaks Bicycle Museum, 616-756-3361

Lemon Creek Fruit Farms, 616-471-1321

Tabor Hill Winery, 616-422-1161

3

Short and Sweet

(M-99)

Getting there: From Detroit, take I-94 west 80 miles to Jackson and turn south on U.S. 127, which runs parallel to M-99. Drive south 40 miles to the Ohio border; take Ohio 20 about 12 miles west to M-99 and turn north. The trip runs south to north.

Getting there: From Toledo, Ohio, take I-90 west and exit at Montpelier, Ohio, to Ohio 15 north, which becomes M-99 when it crosses the Michigan border.

Getting there: From West Bend, Indiana, take I-90 east, exiting at Montpelier, Ohio, and drive north on Ohio 15, which becomes M-99.

Highlights: Lovely small towns to wander; Marshall, the Honolulu House, the Magic Museum, the colleges at Hillsdale and Albion, 19th-century architecture, the capitol building at Lansing.

I used to know a lot about M-99. As a student at Hillsdale College, I hiked the five miles from Hillsdale to Jonesville. On a bike I did the extra miles up to Litchfield or followed 99 south to the Ohio state border, where the number changed to 15. It was also a quick road to Lansing.

You can't go home or back to college days again, but there is a rapport with old roads as with old friends. And it's nice when they still look good.

Driving it recently I saw changes: new business where an old one faded, suburbs where there were none before. But one thing is the same—M-99 is access to wonderful country road explorations. In the checkerboard rural world of south central Michigan, M-99 makes the right moves around some of the prettiest farms and towns in the state.

Hillsdale County's share of the road will get you from the Ohio line to the county seat at Hillsdale in short order, but explore a few back roads first. Wander west toward Camden and Reading and turn onto Carpenter Road, where chances are an Amish buggy or two will bounce nimbly across a side road here in plain-folk farmland.

Once in a long while they come into Hillsdale, a town with a classic 19th-century courthouse in the middle of a square. Old downtown stores have been restoring their rightful heritage look, spruced-up Victorian. This old community of about 7,000 puts on a late-summer county fair that's a dozen notches above average. Saturday auctions at the fairgrounds are sources of furniture bargains if you are shrewd and discerning.

Crowning the highest hill in town, Hillsdale College has won national attention by battling the federal government and winning. The nearly 150-year-old school was first to give degrees to women and blacks (decades before affirmative action), first with a women's gym.

When tall elms and spreading maples are in full fall color and the young and the restless jog to class, the campus has a parklike quality. Focus your camera on Central Hall and its grand old cupola, visible for miles. Gardeners need to see the college's Slayton Arboretum in springtime: it's one huge bouquet with a pond in the middle.

At the 32-room 1872 Grosvenor House in Jonesville (he was a lieutenant governor and a banker), some of the furnishings have been returned, giving the annual Victorian Christmas celebration a genuine reality.

Clocks seem to slow down in the Munro House Bed & Breakfast, first brick house in the county and once a station on the Underground Railroad. This is a dwelling that didn't just see history, but pushed it along. Visitors enjoy antique furnishings (even the linens) and lovely gardens, and the inn is close to theater, golf, cross-country skiing, or whatever else interests you.

Northeasterly then to Litchfield and Homer (larger): wide porches on white houses along tree-rich streets, lilac bushes and mid-American wholesomeness like apple-cheeked children giving an impression that life here has to be almost total sweetness. When you stop for lunch, ask if any yard sales or lawn auctions are going on. . . .

The musically inclined might want to detour east to Hanover (via Mosherville Road, a tad north of Litchfield at the golf course, to Mosherville, north of Hanover Road and east again) to visit the Lee Conklin Antique Organ Museum. It houses nearly 100 restored organs dating back to the Civil War, when even humble homes had an instrument gracing their parlors. Back to Pulaski Road north to tiny Concord and the lovely Mann House Museum and gardens, before rejoining M-99.

Half a mile south of Albion and one mile west on Condit Road, Harrison's Orchard and Cider Mill is open from September to the end of the year. Cider, apples, popcorn, and jams to enjoy now; gift boxes to buy and save for the holidays.

Albion, another college town, was founded on the spot where the Kalamazoo River branches in north and south forks. This was a prosperous place in the late 19th century, as

you might guess from the embellished Second Empire commercial buildings downtown. The famous steel Gale plow,
manufactured in Albion by a successful local iron industry,
drew workers from the industrial centers of Europe and gave
the town a multiethnic outlook and cuisine. For a spicy example, Cajun was popular early on, as proved by the Acadian
Fare restaurant. Beer-battered shrimp, cornbread, and black-
ened beef are served in a vintage riverside house on Michigan
Avenue. Reservations advised.

Acknowledged and honored (even by Hillsdale graduates),
Albion College is one of the best private schools in the state.
Their campus three-gallery art center and print collections are
winners.

Take a look at the restored train station (Amtrak stops
here) to pick up travel information, and stop at the Gardner
House Museum on Superior Street, an easy stroll from downtown. Local families have donated a wealth of antiques, and
there are rooms full of additional Albion history notes.

Time for another detour, this one west on Michigan Avenue,
about 12 miles to Marshall.

Thirty-one historic markers dot the lawns of Marshall
where beautiful (there is no other word) 19th-century residences cluster as if they were at a family reunion. Twelve
National Registry sites are among those marked.

This is a walking-tour town, so park near J. Lund's
Museum of Magic on Michigan Avenue in midtown, and
start off.

Over the years, Marshall has had its bad breaks. Hoping
to be named state capital, the town built a governor's house,
then didn't get the assignment. The Michigan Central Railroad
decided to build its yards in Jackson instead of Marshall. The
local gold mine, patent medicine ("pink pills for pale people"),
had to quit because the cure was 90 percent alcohol. Tsk, tsk.
Still, there were enough prosperous days to leave Marshall

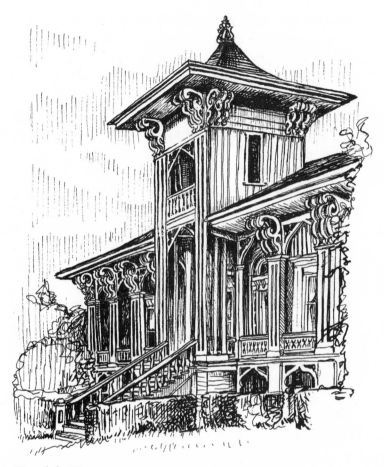

Honolulu House

with a legacy of beautiful houses: Queen Anne, Italianate, Greek and Gothic Revival homes, plus the amazing addition of the "Honolulu House," now a museum.

When Michigan jurist Abner Pratt served as U.S. consul general to Hawaii in 1857, he loved it. Unhappily, his ailing wife longed for home. In an apparent compromise, Pratt returned to Michigan but built a house to duplicate Hawaiian style. A wide veranda to avoid the heat; high-off-the-ground first floor, 15-foot ceilings, open galleries to catch every breeze. He used ebony, teak, and mahogany, then filled his house with coral and tapa cloth, trying to play tropics in the snow. Even though Mr. Pratt must have known the weather well, he refused to face cold facts and died of pneumonia within a few years. A later resident commissioned the intricate frescoes you'll see on tour.

Across the street on Fountain Circle, the National House Inn went up in 1835 as a stagecoach shop and wins the prize as the oldest operating inn in the state. Oozing with country comfort and wonderful smells, the inn's big conversation pieces are the charming garden and the massive beam across the lobby fireplace.

Two more "musts." (I hate lists of "musts"; one person's must is another's big yawn.) But a restaurant wizard named Win Schuler started cooking in a small Marshall hotel dining room, kept expanding till he'd taken over the next-door bowling alley, and blossomed into a chain around the lower peninsula. Schuler's big dinners seldom go wrong.

The American Museum of Magic displays over 250,000 kits, magazines, popping flowers, and tricky boxes for anyone with an ounce of show biz in their makeup (there's that too— clown makeup).

A few miles north of Marshall (you can't miss the signs), the turkeys at Cornwell's farm are a far gobble from the wily birds that Ben Franklin wanted to turn into a national symbol. *These* noble fowl strut handsomely for photos, blissfully unaware that their true appeal is as centerpieces for Thanksgiving tables and as items on Cornwell's Turkeyville restaurant menus. Turkey soup, turkey sandwiches, roast turkey, turkey hash. . . . A petting farm, crafts, a carousel, antiques, and even summer theater are a trot down the path from the turkey sheds that feed the whole operation.

Quickest way to get there from Marshall is via I-69 to exit 48, just a few minutes north of I-94. Then, to get back to

M-99, it's a few zigzags east, back across the freeway and keep going straight.

Low-pressure Eaton Rapids, population 5,000, lives life among the shade trees on the banks of the Grand River. Asked what was unique about her town, one resident replied (after a long and thoughtful pause), "Well now, we have seven bridges across our river." That's a bridge for every 700 citizens; fairly special when you put it to the ratio test.

Then there's the smooth, rich, fruity, sweet, and cold special stuff they dish up at Miller's Ice Cream Parlor and Restaurant. This Miller's is the last of a chain; a good excuse for sundae indulgences.

Now our friendly little road widens to four lanes and enters Lansing as Logan Street, taking you right into the capital area.

The Capitol building recently underwent extensive renovations. Lofty ceilings were long hidden in attempts to tuck more work space beneath them; frescoes and rotunda tiles were dim and cracked. But the 19th-century jewel of Victorian fancy is now totally ready for visitors.

A tall white pine (unreal, but you wouldn't know unless you scratched the bark) stands in the main gallery of the Michigan Historical Museum two blocks west of the Capitol dome. The buildings couldn't possibly be more of a contrast. Michigan's newest capital gain is clean, lean, and almost raw-boned, yet surprisingly warm and welcoming. Its space divides nicely into history museum, state library, and archives with a splendid atrium and another pine tree (real) growing in the center of a masterwork of tile and water. The state tree has seldom been seen amid such class, though it is certainly stately in the forests on its own.

There is much to see in Lansing: the R. E. Olds Museum (cars), Impression 5 (hands-on science), Potter Park Zoo. Take a walk on the boardwalk, several miles long beside the Grand River, or visit the Michigan State University campus, which turns into a living postcard with flowering fruit trees in the spring and brilliant foliage in the fall. The Convention and Visitor's Bureau of Greater Lansing, 119 Pere Marquette between Michigan and Shiawassee downtown, has a spillover bin of ideas.

They are bound to suggest the circle of antique dealers down country roads all around the city or a visit to Grand Ledge, 12 miles to the west, where high cliffs of 270-million-year-old sedimentary rocks add a lot to hiking or biking excursions in Fitzgerald Park.

There's more of everything except M-99.

For More Information

Munro House Bed & Breakfast (Jonesville), 517-849-9292

Mann House Museum (Concord), 517-524-8943

Harrison's Orchard and Cider Mill, 517-629-6647

Acadian Fare Restaurant, 517-629-6827

National House Inn, 616-781-7374

Schuler's Restaurant, 616-781-0600

Marshall Chamber of Commerce, 800-877-5163

Cornwell's Turkeyville, 800-228-4315

Michigan Historical Museum (Lansing), 517-373-3559

R. E. Olds Museum, 517-372-0422

Impression 5 Museum, 517-485-8116

Lansing Chamber of Commerce, 517-487-6800

4

From Lake to Shining Lake

(M-46)

Getting there: From Chicago or Gary, take I-94 to I-196 to M-31 north along Lake Michigan and pick up M-46 just outside Muskegon, 100 miles north of the state line. The trip runs west to east.

Getting there: From Detroit, take I-94 north to Port Huron, follow M-25 along Lake Huron, and pick up M-46 at Port Sanilac, 80 miles from downtown Detroit. Note: This puts you at the east end of the trip; the trip runs west to east.

Highlights: Visit the Hackley house, fruit orchards and farmland, Alma bagpipes, Saginaw roses, and a genuine Japanese teahouse.

Running straight-edge (most of the way) across the center of the lower peninsula, M-46 makes no big promises. It barely touches two small lakes, doesn't skim past any state parks, has to endure the traffic of two cities, and is dead broke on lofty vistas and scenic overlooks.

But if you are standing on one shining shore (Lake Michigan) and hanker for the other one (Lake Huron), M-46 is a good way to go. The keen-eyed country cruiser who doesn't need to cross the state before dinner and *Wheel of Fortune*

can find treasures (even a piece of Japan) and big-sky beauty
along the way.

To start from the western shining lake, one should visit
Muskegon State Park on the shores of Lake Michigan. Put
both feet in the surf along the three miles of perfectly wonderful beach. Popular as a free lunch in summer, this park
boasts a luge run, one of only four in the United States. (The
others are in Marquette, Michigan's Olympic training center;
Lake Placid, New York; and Alaska.) Come properly bundled
up in winter and you, too, can drop-kick downhill through
devilish twists and turns.

Take Memorial Drive around Muskegon Lake into the
downtown area before heading east on M-46.

Muskegon dubs itself "Lumbertown," and it certainly
was. In the 19th-century frenzy of blind consumption, 47
Muskegon sawmills went about leveling forests like human
lawn mowers; Mother Nature went into shock. By 1890 the
trees were gone, the mills closed. A town that once had 40 mil-
lionaires and more silk hats per capita than any other city in
the country went broke. However, one doughty survivor of
these disastrous times was Charles Hackley, who put his
energy into bringing Muskegon back, and his name is all over
a grateful city.

Don't leave without seeing Hackley's fantastic house on
Webster Street (U.S. 31) and that of his partner and next-door
neighbor, Thomas Hume. A showpiece of all the things you
can do with wood, the Hackley house is Victorian
flamboyant: round arches, turrets, multiple fireplaces, and an absent-minded porte cochere
that put the horse under the roof while pas-
sengers scrambled up unprotected steps.
The Hume house is a mite more controlled.
Both are part of a historic district and within
walking distance of the art museum, library, Muskegon

County Museum, and the Visitor's Bureau (in a former school) where you'll find reasons not to hurry out of Muskegon too quickly.

One such reason is the submarine, USS *Silversides*, tied up in Pere Marquette Park. A lucky survivor of the Pacific in World War II, its crew sank 90,000 tons of enemy shipping and can tell tales that movies have been made of.

Or visit the state's biggest amusement park (about as far from a country road as you can get), or take in one of the scheduled laser light shows in Heritage Park.

Back a few blocks, M-46 turns into Apple Avenue and goes near the farmers' market (Tuesday, Thursday, Saturday); or try Wednesday's flea market at 700 Yuba, off Business 31 and Eastern Avenue.

M-46 becomes Laketon Road, then 17 Mile Road for a while, before jogging north on the back of U.S. 131. Swing off through Cedar Springs, a pretty little community whose citizens like to flaunt their red flannel underwear, drop-seats and all. Since the establishment of a red flannel factory years ago, Cedar Springs has been *the* place to go for fall color with a difference. Red Flannel Day comes in early October, with a big one-color parade and everyone in bright long johns or granny gowns.

At Howard City (exit 118 from U.S. 131) the friendly acres of Watts Orchard welcome you at the southwest corner of the village limits. Mouthwatering aromas and colorful displays of tart and sweet cherries all ready for freezing or canning, peaches, plums, apples, apricots, cider, and veggies. The orchard stand is open from early July until November.

You could push your car from here back to M-46 (not advised) to get to the next pig-out—on Colby, cheddar, or Monterey Jack at the Farm Country Cheese House, a smidgeon south of Lakeview on M-91.

Heading east again on M-46, the scenery alternates between woods and farms, and you could do a study of barns as you approach the outskirts of Alma. Now picture this: Bagpipes whine to a stop. Kilted dancers pause and watch. Crowds hush as a man with the heft of two gladiators lifts a tree-trunk-size pole with a grunt and gives it a solid heave. Homesick Scotsmen, ersatz Scotsmen, and folks without a drop of MacDougall in them give a cheer. They have just witnessed the caber throw at the Highland Festival and Games, a Memorial Day weekend tradition in Alma.

This small town has been called "Scotland, U.S.A." Every tartan on the charts is present and accounted for. Parades, floats, athletic events, Highland fling competitions; the festival is a good time that affects the town all year in gift-shop tams, plaid trims, and mountains of Lorna Doones.

When it is not preparing for the games, hosting the games, or toasting the results with Haig & Haig, the community (home to Alma College) offers self-tutored courses in the great outdoors via nature trails in Pine River Park.

Much smaller St. Louis, a little farther on, is like a suburban village amid the farmland. Ask about seeing the Indian cemetery that dates back to 1848 and the Elwell Mansion, an elegant relic from 1883. (It is a sad note that anybody might need to be reminded that a cemetery is sacred ground.)

Barns, grain elevators, and long hills of sugar beets near the railroad tracks (which M-46 seems to keep crossing) mark the road's approach to Saginaw. At Breckenridge a World War II fighter plane is mounted at combat angle in front of a veteran's hall; clustered silos form the village skyline.

Coming into Saginaw from the west on a two-lane road and not an expressway means the fast-food/motel concentrations are in other parts of the city. M-46 seems to arrive suddenly in Saginaw, in an ideally convenient part of town for choice Saginaw sights. One, on M-46 just before you turn north on Washington Street, is the Saginaw Rose Garden.

A rose is a rose is something else when a thousand bushes and 60 varieties are massed around a fountain (recycled water, they want you to know) and bronze sculptures. A floral wonderland, free to all comers. For that price, it's time to stop and smell the roses.

Turn north on Washington a block and a half to the Georgian-style Montague Inn, a bed-and-breakfast straight out of a magazine spread. This was the home of Robert Montague, a beet sugar pioneer who also developed a beet byproduct cosmetic that was eventually sold to the Jergens Company.

Nothing was left out of the Montague house. Library, formal rooms, secret rooms, romantically tucked-away bedrooms with their own fireplaces. In the baths, Pewabic tile, a colorful Michigan product adorning the Detroit Institute of Art and other classic buildings. Oil paintings, Oriental rugs; everything you've ever felt a need for plus eight acres of parklike grounds. Guests have health club privileges, can hold a conference, can be left alone.

Waiting almost next door is an experience available in only five places in America—a genuine Japanese tea ceremony in a teahouse made to Japanese specifications. *Chado*, the way of tea, and *Chanoyu*, the formal ceremony, are not just a matter of pouring refreshment for a friend, but an intricate ballet in which every step, nod, and hand movement follows a traditional pattern. It's a sharing between two people at a special moment (sunset, during a full moon, on a wedding day) in which the tea itself is nearly incidental.

All this came to Saginaw through a sister-city relationship with Tokushima, Japan. A Friendship Garden was planted in 1970, and an authentic Japanese Cultural Center and teahouse came next. The construction of the teahouse, including tatami floor mat and untreated woods, will interest anyone who has ever put two boards together.

Take a long look at the little garden bridge. That's become one of the most popular spots around for bowing in to marriage, and now averages 50 weddings a year.

There is a modest charge to attend the monthly teatime (second Sunday; reservations advised), a lesser fee for a teahouse tour with sweets, and no charge to enjoy the garden.

That tall Gothic structure across Court Street (but still on the same side of Washington) is not a branch of the University of Michigan, but a waterworks plant with one of the best-looking exteriors in the history of pumping stations. Feel free to step inside and look around at the forces behind the city's sinks and bathtubs. (Guided tours are available.) At Christmas the building is festooned with 12,000 lights, luring folks miles out of their way to see it.

There are other Saginaw spots to know about: the area's largest antique mall (70 dealers) on Titabawassee and M-84 north; a grand ex–post office that's now a county museum at 500 Federal Avenue. They just don't make government buildings to look like French châteaus any more.

The Saginaw Visitor's Bureau at 901 South Washington Street has enough brochures on area attractions to paper three barns.

Past I-75, M-46 goes back to its straight and narrow country ways through rich Saginaw Valley farmland. A valley? See if you can find a dip. The land drains toward the Saginaw River and if that makes for a valley, so be it.

Richville, Kingston, Elmer—crossroad clones, friendly and small. Sandusky serves as Sanilac County seat and site of the county fair, an agri-biz extravaganza. The biggest pumpkins I ever saw in my life were here; enough to make a cynical kid believe in that bit about Peter putting his wife into one.

Finally, Port Sanilac on beautiful Lake Huron. (More about the town in Chapter 6.) To make the trip complete, go down to the beach, take off your shoes, and wade. Or ice fish if we're in a different season.

Another world wonder; another wide and shining sea.

For More Information

Muskegon State Park, 616-744-3480

Hackley and Hume Historic Site, 616-722-7578

USS *Silversides*, 616-755-1230

Muskegon Chamber of Commerce, 616-722-3751

Alma Highland Games Information, 517-463-8979

Montague Inn, 517-752-3939

Japanese Cultural Center, 517-759-1648

5

West Side Stories

(M-40 and M-22)

Getting there: From Detroit to pick up M-40, take I-94 west to Marshall, drive south on I-69 to the U.S. 12-Coldwater exit west, and pick up M-86 just outside of town to begin this trip. Colon, the first stop, is about 15 miles west of Coldwater. You will be working your way northwest on Michigan routes 86, 60, and 40 to Holland and Lake Michigan.

Getting there: From Ohio, Indiana, or Chicago to pick up M-40, drive north across the Michigan border on I-69 from I-80/90 in Indiana, take the U.S. 12-Coldwater exit west, and pick up M-86 just outside of town. You will be working your way northwest on Michigan routes 86, 60, and 40 to Holland and Lake Michigan.

Highlights: M-40 works its way northwest from near the Indiana border to Holland and Lake Michigan. Highlights include a magic factory; fruit and wine country; a toy train factory; antiques in Allegan; Holland's windmills, tulips, and wooden shoes; and Saugatuck and Douglas on Lake Michigan.

Highlights: M-22 skirts Lake Michigan in the Traverse City area. Highlights include beaches, fruit farms (especially cherries), Sleeping Bear Dunes National Lakeshore, a lighthouse museum, arts

and crafts, and the Interlochen Center for the Arts and National
Music Camp.

We start off on westbound M-86 to Colon in St.
Joseph County, not too far from the Indiana border
and U.S. 12. There is good reason for this normal-
looking town to have the spirit of Blackstone hovering in its
treetops. Colon is the home of Abbott's Magic Company,
where things you see aren't real, and things you don't see take
shape before your eyes.

Amazements and incredibilities, manufactured and sold
by owner Greg Bordner and his staff, are demonstrated every
Saturday at 1 P.M. during the summer months. They also lead
the wand-waving at Colon's annual Magic Get-Together the
first weekend in August, when magicians from around
America or out of this world try the latest stunts. Buy a trick
for two dollars—or for several thousand if you want to make
a horse vanish during a Broadway show. "We have a magician
on duty from 9 to 5 everyday." Presto change-o: where did
my car go?

M-86 leads to M-60, then we turn north on M-40 and head
deep into fruit country. Two and a half miles north of
Marcellus (*small* town), B & J's Blueberry Ranch and Farm
Market has the berry-pickers' work lined up: blue ones, cur-
rants, gooseberries, red, black, purples. U-pick or they will.
They've already done up the jams and jellies, colorful and
delicious.

Paw Paw presides as unofficial wine capital of the state.
The seat of Van Buren County, it's a town with a courthouse
and an above-average number of businesses. St. Julian Wine
Company (oldest), Warner Vineyards, and the Frontenac
Vineyards (largest, a little bit west of Red Arrow Highway) all
have tasting rooms and tours, and they get together for a gala

wine and harvest festival in the fall. Keep going on Red Arrow and you'll find a golf course and a very big outdoor flea market on summer weekends just beyond it.

A few miles north of Paw Paw, you might enjoy detouring (west on M-43) to Bangor to visit the toy train factory that has taken over a quaint Victorian depot, an appropriate change of roles. There are trains for sale and trains for watching; a gold mine for model railroad enthusiasts.

Back on M-40 head on up to Allegan, another county seat amid farms and woods, astride the Kalamazoo River and on the edge of a 45,000-acre state game area where 10,000 to 20,000 Canada geese spend the winter. Allegan is older than the state and protective of its heritage. The Pioneer Village and Old Farmer's Museum are growing in size and quality at the county fairgrounds, while totally charming old houses on shady side streets keep getting new coats of paint. The Allegan Antique Market, western Michigan's old-but-good champ, is held rain or shine by 300 dealers at the fairgrounds the last Sunday of May, June, July, August, and September.

Stay around at the Winchester Inn on Marshall Street, an 1863 neo-Italianate house with 12-foot ceilings, a green marble fireplace, and a rare hand-poured iron fence. Victorian to the teeth, but very homey. Or choose the Delano Inn Bed & Breakfast, 302 Cutter Street, which is on the National Register of Historic Homes.

Not far away, Holland's kitchens and old-world comforts evoke other voices, other country roads. DeZwaan, a 200-year-old working windmill, once stood in Dutch farmland. With arms reaching to 12 stories, the graceful mill was used as a sniper's roost during World War II and is the last authentic old wind-catcher to be allowed out of the country. Guides in traditional Dutch country clothes will explain. A Dutch country bridge, gardens, and carousel are part of Windmill Island's sprightly complex.

At three-quarter size, the Dutch Village on U.S. 31 also has European country credentials; it's interesting and fun. Real Dutch cuisine and atmosphere are served at the Village Queen's Restaurant, and the huge Dutch-inspired spread behind the village is a discount mall where all the buildings had to conform to the local (that is, Dutch) image.

The third most popular event in the United States—after the Rose Bowl and Mardi Gras—is the Tulip Festival in May in Holland, Michigan. You can have wooden shoes made to order for the occasion, which is an apple-cheeked mindblower of clean family fun. You'll want to tour Baker's Furniture Museum, the Netherlands Museum, and the Delftware and Wooden Shoe factories. And leave the klompen dancing to them.

Take the back roads or U.S. 31 south to Saugatuck and Douglas, two villages occupying a scenic notch between high Lake Michigan dunes. Saugatuck's flair for art and classy old-money houses (half of them are now bed-and-breakfasts) has made it an elite resort town for decades. The ss *Kewatin*, anchored in Douglas, belonged to that proud Great Lakes cruise-ship era. Tiny cabins, but who cared when there was so much mahogany and stained glass? A small fee is charged to go on board and look around.

Sightseeing river cruises, charter fishing boats, and guides to tell you just what's waiting down the area's country roads are all available for your traveling pleasure.

From Detroit or Chicago to pick up M-22, drive to Grand Rapids. Take U.S. 131 north from Grand Rapids about 100 miles. Exit at Kalkaska and drive west on M-72 to Traverse City and Empire, where you can pick up M-22. (Traverse City is 138 miles north of Grand Rapids.)

Michigan's mitten has a little finger as well as a thumb. The Leelanau County peninsula, our green pinkie, extends about 30 miles into the blue world of Lake Michigan and requires a whole new set of adjectives: idyllic, sympatico, eye music, becalming. Within one small county are the splendid Sleeping Bear Dunes, a hundred miles of shore, access to the Manitou Islands, the oldest lighthouse on the lakes, long verdant hills, vineyards, orchards, and vistas that could deplete the state's film supply all by themselves.

Sadly, Leelanau is one of those wonderland areas endangered by its own appeal.

A hundred-plus years ago there were Indian colonies, settler farms, lumbermen, fishermen, and a scattering of summer homes built by families from Detroit or Chicago. Beaches, fruit farms, and loveliness remain, but there's also a sprinkling of condo sites, and fish net reels are mostly props for picturesque shanties turned into boutiques.

Take M-22 from Empire to Sleeping Bear Dunes National Lakeshore park headquarters (a pin-neat town with a waterfront park) and go north to Pierce Stocking Drive—not just a road, an experience. Wherever parking is allowed, get out and climb the boardwalks for dazzling views. In an Indian legend, a mother bear with two cubs swam Lake Michigan to escape a fire. Mama got to shore and fell asleep waiting for her cubs. The cubs drowned, but the Great Spirit Manitou turned mother into a giant dune and the cubs into islands so the mother would never lose sight of them.

M-22 curves north past the chic pleasantries of Glen Arbor, up to Leland where "Fishtown" recalls past industries and there's a ferry boat to Manitou Island. Try the Cove Restaurant beside the dam-created waterfall, ice cream from the corner vendor, or smoked whitefish and fillets from Carlson's. Imported jewelry is sold farther up the street.

On the county's north tip, the Grand Traverse Lighthouse Museum allows visitors up into the 47-foot towers. This is a great area for finding Petoskey stones, coral clusters from an ancient sea that have become Michigan's state stone.

Northport has some inviting bed-and-breakfast stops and first-rate art galleries. In Eddie Joppich's Bay Street Gallery, the prize-winning artist has concentrated on other Michigan painters and sculptors with great success. The Old Mill Pond Inn, Hutchinson's Garden, North Shore Inn, Plum Lane Inn, Vintage House . . . plan to stay in town a while.

Take a jog down road 626 west of Omena to Leelanau Wine Cellars, where you can go on a plant tour and sip samples of wine and champagne.

Old-timers who haven't been to Suttons Bay for 20 years may not recognize the place. Tidied up from former migrant fruit-picking days, Suttons Bay thrives on summer theater, antiques, tall elms, and an appetite for culture. Pack a picnic and a couple of empty buckets, and detour inland on M-204 toward Lake Leelanau in the peninsula's center, then south on 641. A quarter-mile from rejoining M-22, turn north to the end of a dirt road and Flying Scott's Farm. You can fill the buckets with sweet and tart cherries and enjoy your picnic right here; Scott has the tables ready between July 10 and the first weekend in August.

During harvest times or in the spring when fruit trees are in bloom, the hills and sky-filled waters of this area are too good to miss.

A stack of Traverse City area suggestions are available at the visitors center, Grandview Parkway on the Bay. Country devotees will want to swing up U.S. 31, two miles north of the M-72 junction, to Amon's Orchards: see-'em-made cherry products, U-pick fruits, "fruit-mobile" orchard tours May through February. South again half a mile (yes, you passed it), lend an ear to the Music House's collection of automated musical instruments including a huge Belgian dance hall organ. Listening to Gershwin play "Rhapsody in Blue" on a player piano roll that he cut himself is spookily real. Lunch in the Trillium Restaurant 18 floors high at the Grand Traverse Resort charges modestly for a priceless view.

South of town (U.S. 31 to County Road 137), the Interlochen Center for the Arts (all year) and National Music Camp (summers) are a phenomenal success story. Walk through a beautiful part of the Pere Marquette State Forest to hear a student body of rare talent at practice, or drop quietly into a rehearsal hall. Admission is charged for concerts and shows, but you may hear someone like Itzhak Perlman or even the Oak Ridge Boys.

The best things have gone to pots in Karlin, still farther south on CR-137. Frank Ettawageshik and his wife, Mary Anne, make carefully researched Indian pottery from local clays, using no paints, tools, or firing means that weren't available several hundred years ago. Their Pipigwa Gallery has batik, stuffed animals, weaving, and (of course) pottery. An enthusiastic talker, Frank and his pots have been welcomed in ethnic museums from Lansing to St. Petersburg.

From Karlin go west on Betsie River Road and north to CR-608 west through Benzonia to visit Gwen Fostic, a white-haired living Michigan legend who has turned her gift for simple, observant prints of birds, trees, and animals into an industry. A large shop window reveals old Heidelberg presses doing their one-sheet-at-a-time jobs, making wall prints and imprinting stationery and place mats. An ardent conservationist, Fostic has a woodland studio with a freeform grace that brings animals to the door.

The finale for the M-22 trip waits for you at Frankfort, on the edge of Lake Michigan, where sunset-watching from the breakwater provides respite for body and soul.

For More Information

Abbott's Magic Company, 616-432-3235

B & J's Blueberry Ranch and Farm Market, 616-396-3185

St. Julian Winery, 616-657-5568

Warner Vineyards, 616-657-3165

Bangor Train Factory and Museum, 616-427-7927

Allegan Chamber of Commerce, 616-673-2479

Winchester Inn, 616-673-3621

Delano Inn Bed & Breakfast, 616-673-2609

Windmill Island, 616-396-5433

Queen's Inn at Dutch Village, 616-393-0310

Holland Chamber of Commerce, 616-392-2389

Cove Restaurant, 616-256-9034

Manitou Island Ferry, 616-256-9061

Northport Area Chamber of Commerce, 616-386-5806

Traverse City Area Chamber of Commerce, 616-947-5075

Amon's Orchards, 616-938-9160

Music House Museum, 616-938-9300

Grand Traverse Resort, 800-748-0303

Interlochen Center for the Arts, 616-276-9221

Gwen Fostic Prints, 616-882-5505

6

Thumbing, Michigan Style
(M-25)

Getting there: Pick up M-25 at Port Huron, at the foot of Lake Huron, about 60 miles northeast of Detroit. Or, cross the Blue Water Bridge from Sarnia, Ontario, to pick up M-25 in Port Huron. This trip follows a circle from east to west around the Thumb.

Highlights: Lake Huron and all its glories, Port Huron, lake traffic and lighthouses, Sanilac, farm country, beaches and parks along the lake, fishing and birding, a summer of festivals, Bay City, Frankenmuth.

The geographic bulge that makes Michigan's map look like a big mitten could only have one nickname. Say "Thumb" and everyone knows you're headed for farm and field country close to a serene shore. You're going to be doing a little fishing, attend the Sugar Festival, or buy veggies so fresh the pickers are still washing their hands.

Just about an hour (by expressway) from downtown Detroit or Lansing, the need to keep revving into higher gear vanishes; coasting takes over. Four-lane highways don't make it into the Thumb, stop signals are curiosities, and only grain silos need elevators.

Just where this tranquil digit begins is up for friendly debate but most of us settle for a loose line running from Port Huron to Bay City. The tip, Port Austin, is only 124 miles from Detroit's city hall.

A grid of beeline country roads covers the sub-peninsula, where enough beets and beans are grown to make this part of the United States a champion producer of white navy beans and beet sugar. There are  woods and a few secluded inland lakes, but it's the flat, wide square miles of farmland that typify the landscape.

M-25 outlines the Thumb and gives it a feel for visitors; M-19, M-53, and other interior roads are working tendons. Zigzag around a bit for the best of the Thumb. Motels cluster along the western edge (mostly), but the number of bed-and-breakfasts is growing, and nothing is too far away for a prudent phone call. Photo note: If this has to be a swift one-day jaunt (two or three days are much better), start early in Port Huron to catch the sun on the eastern shore, then the right light will be waiting as you reach the west side.

Sitting where Lake Huron meets the St. Clair River, Port Huron gets it both ways. South- or northbound freighters from around the world silently enter or leave the upper Great Lakes, while the two side-by-side Blue Water Bridges feed travelers east and west, in and out of Canada. "Crossroads" or "gateway" applies here.

Visit Port Huron's Museum of Art and History on Sixty Street if you're in town at the right hour, or the little red depot tucked nearly under the bridge where Thomas Edison used to be a newsboy. A long promenade on the waterfront for hiking and freighter-gazing has a former Coast Guard lightship, now a small museum, tied up at the north end. A river full of smaller craft runs through the center of town.

A grand view of everything is yours with lunch at the Fog Cutter Restaurant on the sixth floor of the Port Huron Office Center on Fort Street, close to the river. Sarnia, Ontario, can be seen across the stream. After dark a zillion lights on Sarnia's huge petrochemical plant present a show of their own.

To build a small Thumb reference library, stop at the Michigan Welcome Center, 2260 Water Street and I-96 for lists of pick-your-own orchards, farms, fairs, fish, flora, and fauna. Include antique dealers and pie shops.

At Omar and Garfield streets, north of the bridge, the regal Fort Gratiot Light reigns over a Coast Guard station. A small park lets you get close enough for photos. This was the earliest lighthouse on Lake Huron and is the oldest surviving light in Michigan. Built in 1825, when 66 feet seemed wondrous tall, an extra 20 feet had to be added in 1861. The white brick structure (first object in the state to be touched by the rising sun) with adjacent keeper's home has been a vital navigation aid for a lake bigger than Connecticut, Vermont, and New Hampshire combined.

M-25 used to leave Port Huron and that was it—instant change of ambience. Not now. Mushrooming suburbs, malls, and fringe benefits like fast food carry big-town echoes to Lakeport and slightly beyond.

It makes Lakeport State Park (315 campsites) seem empty.

Lakeport, Port Sanilac, Port Hope. Long ago they *were* ports—shipping lumber, grindstones, and other Michigan products. Then the Thumb's pine forests were hit in 1871 and 1873 by devastating fires that ripped across the state, taking lives, hundred of buildings, and most of the trees. (1871 was also the year Mrs. O'Leary's lantern-kicking cow started the Chicago fire, and scores of people also died in Wisconsin blazes.)

The economy turned to farming and shipping fish.

Another change came with a lethal storm in 1913. Eight freighters went down in nearby waters taking all on board, dozens of other ships were wrecked, and all coast docking facilities were wiped out. Ports had to struggle into a new era.

Farms and produce on one side of the road and the second largest Great Lake on the other (often hidden by private cottages), M-25 becomes more "country" with each mile north.

At Lexington turn right at the light, pass a block of neat boutiques and freshly painted storefronts to make personal contact with water, sand, picnic tables, and strollable breakwaters. The table should have something from a local baking wizard's oven (i.e., Mary's Pie Shop) to make the setting perfect. A privately owned authentic lighthouse can be seen (but not toured) a block to the south.

Now a little detour. Follow M-90 west past the golf course, turning near a sugar beet processing plant into Croswell. Those huge piles of whitish roots are beets containing at least 12 percent sugar . . . which is hard to imagine if you ever bit into one. Another sweet success in Croswell is the Berry Farm Market and Ice Cream Parlor, where you can pick your own or buy succulent strawberries, blueberries, raspberries (in season, naturally), or jars of jam. It's just six blocks west of midtown, at 33 Black River Road; in Croswell that's far enough to be back on the farm.

One odd nearby attraction is the "mother-in-law bridge" across the narrow Black River. Someone put up a rope-and-board suspension bridge, maybe to reach or escape from a mother-in-law, and this modest achievement in the annals of engineering has gotten far more publicity than it deserves. However, a sign on M-25 and a stream of referrals to it have made the span famous.

Back on M-25, a Victorian mansion on Port Sanilac's south side doubles as the Sanilac Historical Museum. The handsome yellow Empire-style house amid its coterie of pine trees was built by the region's first doctor, Joseph Loop, and used by his descendants for 92 years. The doctor's office and his prosperous family's furnishings are still there. Grandson S. G. Harrison, naturalist, adventurer, and Great Lakes ship captain, added his marine collection, military regalia, and Indian crafts; there's lots to browse through and admire.

Out in back, peer into a pioneer barn and cabin, visit the dairy museum (the Thumb could have been called the "milkpail"), and check out the extremely successful summer theater. Everything closes up between October and mid-June, though, so timing is important.

Port Sanilac's waterfront offers good fishing from long breakwaters. Years ago the state established "Harbors of Refuge" every 30 miles along the coast, and these bulwarks are among the results.

Another classic house built by a founding father has become a bed-and-breakfast. At 111 South Ridge Street, the red brick Raymond House Inn, circa 1871, has those high ceilings, a winding staircase, and other features we will always love.

Tiny shoreline communities go by almost without notice, but you can't miss Harbor Beach. If the name Frank Murphy rings bells, good for you. Murphy was born here. Supreme Court justice, Detroit judge, state governor, governor general of the Philippines, attorney general. He endeared himself to Michigan labor when, as governor, he refused to call in troops to stop a Flint autoworkers' strike. A tiny museum on M-25 is full of Murphy mementos.

Harbor Beach has a lot of parks for a town its size. Most face the harbor, an inlet often claimed to be the largest manmade harbor in the country.

West of Harbor Beach is the Huron County seat, Bad Axe, home of the Thumb tip's only daily newspaper. Worth seeing is the quaint collection of pioneer log cabins that fills one corner of the city park. There's also theater, a golf club, and a lively county fair in late August.

Double back to catch the next coastal beacon on M-25 at Lighthouse Park, where the land begins to curve west. The light is not open to the public, but as it towers over the trees with blue Lake Huron behind, it is posed for a nice photo.

Next, the Pioneer Huron City Museum's assorted buildings include an 1885 Coast Guard lifesaving station, complete with lifeboat and bell. Station crews were a hardy, courageous breed, rowing their little craft against the often icy seas to rescue men from foundering vessels. In the museum are tales of unsung heroes, a country store with lore, bric-a-brac under glass, and easy history lessons. Also on the grounds is the church where famed Yale professor William Lyons Phelps's summertime sermons necessitated a steady stream of building additions. His home, "The House of Seven Gables," can be seen but not toured. The museum area is open in July and August only.

In 1834 rock of whetstone quality was found around the Thumb tip, and a business of knife sharpeners and millstones flourished for the next hundred years. The biggest stone made here was over three tons. Grindstone City has ground down from its maximum population of 600 to a family-sized enclave of small cottages with the remnants of those long-gone times being used for decorative signs and borders. Grindstone City is an ultra-pleasant fishing spot.

The road slides quickly into Port Austin, popular day-trip destination and cottage town. Out on the wide breakwater, dedicated fisherfolks can watch the sun come up and then watch it set. If an urge to try a little deep-water trolling takes over, there are enough charter boat operators around this area to man the *Queen Elizabeth II*.

On Lake Street, i.e., the road to Bad Axe, sits a trio of very special bed-and-breakfasts. The Garfield Inn (a president slept here), a National Historic Site, is a beguiling place for dinner. Across the street, the Lake Street Inn's high peaked gables and large bay windows shelter a common room with a hot tub in front of a wood stove . . . among other touches, including a gift shop, antiques, sodas, and snacks. Only yards away the Questover Inn, an ample, white frame beauty with wrap-around porch and broad shady lawn, faces the sunset.

Old church pews and a brass teller's cage add charisma to a Port Austin restaurant you can count on—or in. Another National Historic Site, "The Bank" serves gourmet meals in a restored old bank building. Very seasonal and the hours are eclectic; but if you can, invest.

Fresh fish (for those who forgot their tackle box) can be purchased a block west of Lake Street on M-25.

The sunset side of the Thumb is blessed with extra numbers of parks, towns you might like to have been born in, and a greater supply of motels. Bass, perch, trout, salmon, and wall-eye conventions in Saginaw Bay make the Thumb coast as sought-after as ice cream. It's worth doing a bit of motel research and reserving ahead in summer.

Port Crescent and Sleeper State Parks are nearly side-by-side, both hugging acres of breezy beach with soft, fine sand, rare dune grasses, wetlands, and wildflowers. Port Crescent has added an exercise trail to its three miles of hiking paths. Campsites are available, too.

Coast residents love evenings with a deck of cards and a beer, but they love a festival even more. Caseville puts on a Victorian Art Fest and Venetian Night (boat parade) in June, and a Walleye Tournament in July. Bay Port boasts Fish Sandwich Day in August (hundreds sold), and Sebewaing hosts the Sugar Festival in late June. That's the plug-puller where a queen presides and a big parade is the grandest event to hit Huron County all year.

Unlikely little Bay Port once ran the largest freshwater fishing port in the world (it shrank in modern times). If your cooler is ready, you can pick out supper at the Bay Port Fish Company's commercial operation.

Duck hunters and bird-watchers flock to the Saginaw Bay area for its extraordinary concentrations of waterfowl. From the Wildfowl Bay State Wildlife Area near Bay Port around to Nayanquing Point State Wildlife Area, the south end of Saginaw Bay is one marsh and sanctuary after another.

M-25 runs into Bay City, kingpin of Lake Huron commerce. When cutting free trees could make you rich, Bay City ran up a record for shipping four *billion* feet of lumber by 1888. Dramatic houses built by the lumber barons line up on Center Street, while the whole area can be viewed from the tower of the great Romanesque city hall, next to the historical museum. Worthy of note: during World War II, Bay City produced a navy vessel every week.

Concerts in the park, a whopping Fourth of July fireworks display, and boat-watching along the Saginaw River are also among Bay City's charms.

Then back to country roads, such as M-83 south to Frankenmuth, a Bavarian phenomenon founded by determined Frankish immigrants.

With its own beer and a flair for chicken dinners, Frankenmuth is a frothing tourist attraction, but fun to visit. German family cuisine at Zehnder's and the Bavarian Inn has put them among America's 10 most popular restaurants; people come across the state for dinner.

Near a street chock-full of wood-carvers, clock shops, Hummelware, and all things *Deutsche*, you can watch a glockenspiel with Pied Piper figures accompanying the hour chimes three times a day, or walk across an authentic old world–style covered bridge.

Bronner's, which claims to be the world's largest Christmas store, never lets up on its favorite season; their permanent storefront Magi greet nearly as many tour buses as the White House. Every elf, flashing tree, Santa plate, crèche, or styrofoam gingerbread house (is that a mechanized reindeer doing his laundry?) you've ever seen in any store window or catalog can be carried out of Bronner's. In May. Or July. Fifty thousand Christmas selections can do things for your faith.

From here, take the first road east (left, if you're on southbound M-83), then south, then east (pick a road, any road) until you reach M-24 going to Lapeer. Nine miles north of Lapeer and a jog east to the end of Barnes Lake Road, the Apple Barn, Cider Mill, and Farm Market offers U-pick or ready-to-go farm products. Either way, the variety of fruits and vegetables and the sweet ciders of fall are the distilled essence of Thumb country.

Just south of Lapeer, I-69 will scoot you back to Port Huron to complete the circle. But take your time.

For More Information

Museum of Arts and History, 810-982-0891

Fog Cutter Restaurant, 810-987-3300

Port Huron Area Information, 800-852-4242

Sanilac Historical Museum, 810-622-9946

Raymond House Inn, 810-622-8800

Frank Murphy Museum, 517-479-9664

Pioneer Huron City Museum, 517-428-4123

Garfield Inn, 517-738-5254

The Bank Restaurant, 517-738-5353

Bay City Visitor's Bureau, 517-893-1222

Frankenmuth Chamber of Commerce, 517-652-6106

Zehnder's Restaurant, 517-652-9925

Bavarian Inn, 517-652-9941

Bronner's Christmas Store, 800-ALL-YEAR

7

Off on a Mission

(M-37)

Getting there: From Chicago, drive north along Lake Michigan on I-94 and U.S. 31.

Getting there: From Detroit, take I-75 north to Grayling and follow M-72 and U.S. 31 west to Traverse City.

Highlights: This is fruit country—vineyards, Château Grand Traverse Winery, apple and cherry orchards; also glimpses of the lake; Mission Point Lighthouse.

"If you seek a pleasant peninsula, look about you"—Michigan's motto rings with modesty but hits the mark. Sheer pleasantness sings out loud on a narrow strip of territory called Old Mission Peninsula, the ridge dividing Grand Traverse Bay into two arms.

The Mission Peninsula is at the tip of the ring finger of the left hand that is Michigan. The peninsula juts into Grand Traverse Bay in Lake Michigan just north of Traverse City. M-37, Center Road, rides the high spine of this long (18 miles), narrow (one or two miles) land spit; it curves and dips, then rises to wonderful views from both sides of the car. Cherry and apple orchards in every stage of maturity reach to each other across the succession of gentle hills. In spring it is spectacular to see long slashes of bright blue water beyond airy clouds of pink blossoms.

And there are vineyards—acres of vineyards. Land that once was deep under warm primordial seas, then gouged, scraped, compressed, and pushed up by glaciers, now supports this final toast to the good life.

Three Traverse City streets lead into the peninsula from U.S. 31. East Shore Road, Center Road, and Peninsula Drive. They are easy to miss, as there aren't any billboards blaring "Turn! This is it!" The natives would shudder. The peninsula's modern mission is to retain a low-key presence while anchored in the state's fastest-growing tourist area.

Both shore roads lead to Center Road (M-37), Old Mission's Main Street, after a few residential blocks.

On the East Shore, drive between attractive homes and their private docks, meticulous lawns, and sequestered beaches. The road arcs carefully past sailboats at anchor, others under blue tarps or heading out, depending on the time of day and year. When East Shore Drive reaches M-37, houses thin back and farm country takes over.

Underwood's Country Store on McKinley Road stocks the region's bounty: cherry-apple cider, cherry pies, jams, jellies, pailfuls of cherries or bushels of apples. Five minutes away on a breezy hilltop, the Château Grand Traverse Winery raises grapes, distills their essence, and bottles products that astonished the wine world by winning gold medals at international competitions.

This was sweet vindication for wine importer Edward O'Keefe, who was sure that the Mission Peninsula had the right soil and climate for fine European Vinifera wines. In 1976 he established his winery while aficionados snorted. Not any more. O'Keefe's Château Chardonnays, Merlot, Rieslings, and

Pinot Noir demonstrated quality and filled his tasting room wall with prize ribbons and citations.

The Château Grand Traverse Winery stays open from April I through November 30; summer pilgrims can tour the whole facility. What you can't do, however, is buy any wine before noon on Sunday mornings.

Farther along, past Kelly's Roadhouse Café, past the Old Mission Tavern (both loaded with rustic charm and good food), a detour east on Old Mission Road winds around to the founding mini-town of Old Mission. An if-we-don't-have-it-maybe-you-don't-need-it type of general store keeps peace next to a replica of the Presbyterian church built in 1839 for the Chippewa Indians. The little log structure serves as a tiny historical museum, spreading the good and bad news about peninsula history. Visitors "meet" the Reverend Peter Dougherty, mission founder, and learn how this was once the mailbox for the whole area. There are bits on the establishment of cherry farming, pieces on cherry-picking machines displacing migrant workers, and how a ruinous one-crop economy forced diversity.

On Swaney Road and east there's very good family swimming at Haserot's Beach. Shallow, sheltered, and sandy.

Back on M-37, cars skim the west shore up to Old Mission Point Lighthouse Park, with its swimming beach and breeze-swept picnic spot. The cottage-size lighthouse, built in 1870 and primly protected by a picket fence, is no longer open to the public. It served long and well, another reminder of the importance of lights to the development of long-distance traveling on the Great Lakes.

Two well-known shipwrecks lie beneath the waves off Mission Point. The schooner *Metropolis* went under in 1886, and the *A. J. Rogers* sank in 1898. Trivia collectors will also note that they stand near the 45th parallel, halfway between the North Pole and equator. The actual line is out in the water beyond the tip, but an interesting chart shows you where the 45th parallel hits other countries. It is hard to believe that you are standing on a latitude even with Venice, Italy, for example.

If zigzagging down side roads on the return trip reaches a couple of dead ends, that's part of the fun. Take a paved road and it may turn to gravel, then become a dirt lane before you either make a U-turn or suddenly find the concrete again.

With shimmering water beyond every farm or clump of trees, Old Mission scenery never lets you down. On the west side, the extension of a stubby sub-peninsula gives form to Bower's Harbor. Nothing showy here; just a humble little port where motorboats refill snack chests and gas tanks or pick up an evening paper.

Ambling below the speed limit means you've caught on. From here south, Peninsula Drive and the west shoreline stick together. Handsome hillside houses are sensibly walled with windows to let the lucky owners gaze at sailboats, swans, and sunsets with wide-angle vision. (About 400 mute swans nest in the Traverse City area. They look placid, but be cautious or you may discover a ballerina gone mad. Swan pecks are hard to explain back home.)

One of the classiest of old summer homes on the Drive has gained latter-day fame as a superb place for dinner. Bower's Harbor Inn seduces with candlelight, crystal, fireplaces, a romantic view of the bay, and stories about a genteel ghost that shows up occasionally. In the mansion's old coach house (The Bowery) the ambience switches from silk to denim. Tables wear checkered cloths in a rough-hewn balconied space; jazz, rock, and the perfumes of a grill fill all corners.

It is easy to return to M-37 (Center Road) any time, but if the sun is sinking slowly behind the westward hills of Leelanau and sending a gold path across the bay, forget it. You'll get back to U.S. 31 all too soon anyway.

For More Information

Underwood's Country Store, 616-947-8799

Château Grand Traverse Winery, 800-283-0247 or 616-223-7355

Bower's Harbor Inn, 616-223-4222

8

Pursuing the Stately Elk

Pigeon River Country State Forest

Getting there: Take I-75 north and exit at Vanderbilt, 200 miles north of Detroit, almost at the fingertip of the Michigan mitten. Take Main Street east, which turns to gravel. Follow the directions in the text to the headquarters of Pigeon River Country State Forest.

Highlights: Beautiful forest preserve and wildlife worth exploration all year round.

Elk roam (the official word is "range") in a 700-square-mile region of the northeastern lower peninsula, congregating heavily in a core area between Vanderbilt and M-33. On the official state map (hanging behind the glass at interstate rest areas) the route to find them looks simple enough. Exit I-75 at Vanderbilt; a paved road east from town turns to gravel, winds around two tiny silhouettes indicating elk, then joins a second road (paved) curving back to Gaylord or Vienna. Or it's possible to take another gravel path east to paved M-33. . . .

But to view the stately creatures (also called wapiti) may take some searching and wandering around on roads that are *very* country. This is a trip into the Pigeon River Country State Forest, another one of those beguiling areas of deep woods, small lakes, and pristine meadows that Michigan specializes in. (A fall color spectacular!) We are about to explore a country road through a part of Michigan as unspoiled as a new day, although it's a day with possible hazards.

Before going, fill up the gas tank, put more munchies in the picnic hamper, and back out if you have little tolerance for getting lost. The roads have signs, sometimes; they often seem longer than what you were told. A few too many bends on a day with no sun to give you directional clues and driving here can get confusing.

From Vanderbilt's center (at the flashing light) turn east on Main Street, which becomes Sturgeon Valley Road. For eight miles after leaving the city limits the road is blacktop, then it turns to gravel. Pickerel Lake Road leads to a campground; another campground is at Pigeon Brook. The turn not to miss comes at Twin Lakes Road up to forest headquarters.

A handsome log building with attractively shaped double doors and a big fireplace, the headquarters replaces one that burned down a few years ago. Ask all the questions you want about elk and trees and forest uses, but don't leave without a map.

The Pigeon River Country has had some bleak and barren times. First it was logged heavily between 1860 and 1910. Uncontrolled fires swept through in later years, tempting a few hopeful farmers to try to convert the stumpy ground to agriculture. That didn't work but resulted in large parts of the region returning to state ownership because of unpaid taxes and purchases.

These counties and most other areas of the state once had herds of native elk, but they disappeared when the forest habitat was being destroyed and hunting went unregulated. From the Pigeon River Country State Forest folder:

In 1918 seven elk were released near Wolverine. By 1927 they had multiplied to as many as 500. The elk herd now numbers about 1,000 animals. Limited elk hunts are planned to achieve a balance between elk numbers, their environment, agricultural damage, and recreational viewing.

"Recreational viewing" sounds better than "just to look at them," but it does not hint at the recreation you may go through to get in eyeball-to-antlers focus length.

Or to *hear* them. Amid the fall color, persons who pursue elk in September might get to hear the mating season's announcements from bulls: their bugle. Hard to figure just how the elk's sex signals came to be named "bugle" when they sound more like a wheezing Scrooge having a bad day on his bagpipe . . . then grunting in misery. He's telling other bulls to stay away from his girls (usually about 10 to a harem). It's a less-than-charming sound, but it certainly adds fun to the bird calls when you're out in the woods.

Elk viewing areas are all around, some with log posts to prevent the meadows from becoming parking lots. Elk are more apt to be spotted in the evening or very early morning, but they are notorious for not showing up when you have out-of-state visitors in the car. The last time I went through, there were none in sight, although the ranger said about 80 had been seen in the same area the evening before.

The true lover of the outdoors doesn't fret about these things. It is a lovely region for just driving around, maybe stopping to climb a hill or two and look out over the trees. Michigan has more tree species native to the state than any other of the 49. Along these roads the white pine, tamarack, birch, chokecherry, and balsam can be spotted, giving cover to grouse, wild turkeys, and a wide variety of game. In 1985 the forest management reintroduced pine marten, a soft-furred little mammal, and they are doing well.

Drive slowly, especially after dark, when you might catch an elk in the glare of your headlights. Elk are larger and heavier than deer; their coloring runs to tan and chocolate brown. Tails are stubby. Deer, on the other hand, have tan/gray coats and longer tails. A deer polishes off about four pounds of browse per day, but a hungry elk has to have 12 to 16 pounds. Farmers are rightly alarmed when elk get into their orchards.

Adult elk stretch a bit over five feet high (plus antlers), and bulls can reach nearly 1,000 pounds. Cows are a demure 400 pounds or so.

As the forest map will show, the Pigeon River Country State Forest is wrapped in bundles of paved and gravel roads, scenic overlooks, 60 miles of foot paths, 27 miles of horse trails, an endless supply of closed roads, rivers, and streams. Seven campgrounds and more than a dozen lakes are within its boundaries.

As I searched for the elusive elk of November, the snow began to fall. There are no white lines at the edge of gravel roads anyway, and a deep snowfall can obscure everything. My gas was running low. There were no signs when I needed them.

Since I never travel without a sleeping bag and emergency gear in the car, I wasn't worried, but still saw fit to flag down the only truck I had passed in an hour.

"Which way to the nearest gas station?"

"There's nothing the way you're headed. Better follow me." Which I did, making it back to Vanderbilt as the dreaded out-of-gas sputter was about to start.

By next morning a foot of snow had brought ditches to road level and obscured trails. Lovely but possibly lethal if you are without fuel in the backwoods. In lighter snowfalls, it is nice to know that 60 percent of the Pigeon River Country Forest is within a quarter mile of a road and 98 percent is within a mile. Snowplows keep the main lines open.

The treasured elk herd probably won't be allowed to grow any bigger. Deer leaping across the highway are killed by the thousands every year and do enormous damage to cars and drivers. Overcrowded elk on the road seeking new territory would be infinitely worse.

For More Information

For Pigeon River and Mackinaw State Forest information call Gaylord office, 517-732-3541

Gaylord/Otsego Tourism, 517-732-4000

9

North by Northeast

(U.S. 23)

Getting there: From Detroit, take I-75 north, exit at West Branch, pick up M-55, and follow it east to Tawas City on Lake Huron, or exit I-75 at Standish and drive north along the lake on U.S. 23 to Tawas City. This trip runs from south to north and back.

Getting there: From Canada, cross the St. Clair River at Sarnia, take I-69 to Flint, then go north on I-75 and follow the directions above.

Highlights: Sandy beaches and rocky stretches along Lake Huron, fishing, state parks, Lumberman's Monument, canoeing, bicycling, lighthouses, dinosaurs, a limestone quarry, small towns, and festivals.

First you've got to know: socially, physically, and historically the northeastern part of the lower peninsula mitten is not a mirror-image of the northwestern side. Sand dunes are lower, the land is much flatter, towns are smaller, woods deeper; few lakes lie just inside Huron's shore, and there aren't any cities (such as Chicago, Milwaukee, or Gary) to push streams of vacationers across a shared coast.

North Huron's Alpena, another lumber camp that grew to city size, was reachable only by boat in times when crowded trains and busy ferries were weaving webs around Lake Michigan. A paved highway from Detroit to Alpena didn't open until 1937.

The northeast coast of Michigan's Lower Peninsula is not on the way to somewhere else. Going along the sunrise edge will slow down any trip to Saulte Ste. Marie.

What a great place to be. Uncrowded soft-sand beaches and rocky, rugged stretches alternate along the shores. Fishing is bravo, restaurants serve more than you can eat, resorts are big on plain comforts, small on ruffled pillows and lace curtains. The native uniform may be a red plaid shirt with waders or hiking books, but folks can fancy up if it seems worthwhile. They are a warm and friendly bunch.

U.S. 23 is the key route into a country all its own. And whether you approach from West Branch or Standish, you'll cross the Rifle River, a 90-mile stream popular to the point of legend with canoeists.

First stop may be Tawas City and East Tawas, civic siblings that blend into each other without a clear seam. Both have waterfront parks and piers; both share the visitors center at the water's edge. The "water" is a dent in the Huron shoreline known as Tawas Bay.

By midsummer both towns overflow, 450 motel rooms are filled, 14 restaurants (there will be more as soon as I write this) are pouring coffee as if from hoses, and dozens of racing sailboats are whisking across the waves. A shore-to-shore biking/hiking/riding trail to Lake Michigan starts (or ends) in Tawas. Once a year members of the Michigan Trail Riders Association walk their steeds out into the waters of Lake Huron, then head west. If you plan to do a hike, it would be best not to follow this group too soon.

North and west lies the Huron National Forest, once a victim of the ruinous lumbering practices of the last century.

In this region, however, a conservation light was lit when the Kiwanis organization led a reform by planting over a million seedling trees. Ask at the Iosco County Historical Museum for directions to the Lumberman's Monument, and remember the poor jacks who faced their employment stoically for low pay and no benefits, slept in flea-ridden bunks, and often died under falling trees or of early old age. Tree policies were not their doing. Here at the Monument is their thank-you.

Out on a perfectly lovely curl of land the Tawas Point State Park and lighthouse has a two-mile beach and plenty of shade trees. Take time to hike the Sandy Hook Nature Trail, a boardwalk over the fragile dunes with benches for easier bird-watching. As gulls rise to ski down their invisible slopes without a flap of a wing, and red-winged blackbirds warble from

Tawas Point Lighthouse

the tops of cattails, and the winds of a Great Lake swirl around, Tawas Point makes contact with another world.

The Tawas lighthouse is open by appointment to groups with reservations; the 202 camping units are open all year.

Two more close communities, but in no way twins, are Au Sable (one of the smallest townships in Michigan) and Oscoda (one of the largest). They share the Au Sable River, a long, long stream winding through the Huron Forest and flowing with fish tales about trout, coho, racing canoes, and general folklore. Yarns about northwoods lumberman Paul Bunyan and his blue ox, Babe, have been standard fare for generations. Oscoda native James MacGillivary collected them in the early 1900s and gets chief credit for making Paul a national hero.

Every year in late July, tough-it-out canoeists leave Grayling in mid-state and paddle for more than 150 winding miles to Oscoda in a grueling nonstop Au Sable marathon. Two-person teams leave late on a Friday afternoon to paddle through the night. Colliding with tree trunks in the dark while going full speed ahead is the tough part; the fun comes in the cheering for those who make it to Oscoda next morning.

Pleasant, tree-lined, and slightly hilly, U.S. 23 travels the coast behind thick curtains of pine and cedar with quick flashes of blue now and then. You can gaze at it from a roadside park a few miles north of Oscoda, then again from Harrisville State Park or Harrisville's waterfront.

As a harbor of refuge and county seat, Harrisville has no problem drawing a summer crowd. It's usually a happy crowd, but the most cheerful of gatherings anywhere is the annual Harrisville meeting and competition of the Society for the Preservation and Encouragement of Barber Shop Quartets in America (SPEBSQA). The week before Labor Day weekend, SPEBSQA groups begin to assemble, going through their tuneful do-re-mi's on front porches, around tailgates, or out on the beach. By the weekend, "Sweet Adeline" seems like a national anthem of sorts and the musical fun is high-pitched. A big art fair on the courthouse grounds adds to the festivities.

If you've made a reservation far in advance for a night or at least dinner at the Big Paw Resort, you are lucky. Given the AAA's four-diamond rating (right up there with the cuisine of the Grand Hotel on Mackinac Island), this is cooking as Grandma's should have been. About a mile and a half north of Harrisville, Big Paw is down an awkward old logging road between U.S. 23 and the lake; it's rustic, spotless, genial, and deserving of the high praise it gets. Everything is fresh and homemade. No wine.

Past a lighthouse at Sturgeon Point (you must leave U.S. 23 to see it), past a road off to tiny Alcona and Black River, Ossineke looms as a modest little place with Lake Huron beaches, a state forest campground, and scenic side roads that are especially wonderful during the fall color show. And a garden of earthly frights.

Ordinarily I shun anything as touristy as a dinosaur garden, but the one at Ossineke is special. A magnificent stand of trees, labeled and their habits explained, winds along the path. At well-spaced intervals a creature from Earth's earlier days shows up in a menacing stance or in combat (leave it to a Tyrannosaurus rex to make trouble). There are even cavemen finishing off a mammoth. Children love this place, and any adult can appreciate the carefully groomed woodland before hitting the road again.

Towns of size have a simple way of announcing it: they wear malls on the outskirts. Alpena has full-scale shopping on its south side, therefore expect more than you have yet seen on U.S. 23. Expect a city with a wildlife sanctuary within its limits, three city beaches, a daily paper, live theater, and at least 30 places to order dinner. The Jesse Besser Museum runs from art to ancient artifacts to astronomy and touring shows of top caliber. The Besser would be an asset anywhere. Of added interest: philanthropist Besser's house near the lakefront is now a bed-and-breakfast.

Alpena's bay has not been easy on ships. Jagged rocks in all the wrong places along this stretch of coast plus the fierce storms of November (when fresh water freezes quickly around a ship's rigging, a cargo it can't steer with) are historic menaces. The remains of more than 16 "Shipwreck Alley" vessels in the Thunder Bay Underwater Preserve have made diving a big Alpena business.

Think about it over dinner at the Thunderbird Inn while eating fish fresh from the lake you are gazing across. There's golf, there's tennis, but nothing ever outranks fishing in a place with overlapping fishing derbies most of the year.

U.S. 23 skims the east side of Long Lake. Turn at Grand Lake Road and drive to the north end to reach Old State Road and two handsome lighthouses on Presque Isle. Oldest is a stocky-looking light, 30 feet high with walls four feet thick. Stairs of great stone blocks circle up to the top and—as if you were climbing inside a conch shell—the tower echoes softly with sounds of wind and sea.

The keeper's dwelling has been turned into a homey museum with marine and kitchen gear, and the needs for a life apart. Punishment stocks out in back are a bit of a puzzle, but fun for picture-taking.

About a mile north, a second "new" light tower took over for the old one in 1871. Recently restored, it's 113 feet tall.

At the junction with M-65, plans may vary. U.S. 23 goes on, of course, to Rogers City, Cheboygan, Mackinaw City, and a great beautiful highway into space, the Mackinac Bridge (which is longer than the Golden Gate). For a shorter trip, go south on M-65, then back to M-55 or U.S. 23 when they meet again.

Looping up and then back down U.S. 23, here's what you don't want to miss: Rogers City's limestone quarry. Not just *any* limestone quarry, but the world's largest. Watch the dynamiting operation at the quarry, then see stone sorted, freighters loaded.

Fresh fish at bargain prices at the Gauthier and Spaulding retail outlet, one of Michigan's few remaining commercial fisheries. Smoked pork loin, a favorite item here since 1913, comes out of Plath's Meats smokehouse. Have them wrap a piece to take home, then feast like family in Kortman's Restaurant. Plain good.

P. H. Hoeft State Park's glorious acres of sand and trees and more of the same at the Cheboygan State Park. In Cheboygan (gateway to a lot of inland lakes), the 100-year-old opera house has been restored and sponsors special events all year round.

At Old Mill Creek State Historic Park (three miles south of Mackinaw City) a carefully restored sawmill shows how a little stream of water can be harnessed to drive a giant saw blade through huge logs. Much more to see and enjoy at this historic site with flair. Then at Mackinaw City, a wonderfully restored fort—more history done with drama and craft—fudge kitchens and ferries to Mackinac Island (see Chapter 14). Plus enough motel space to house the Rose Bowl crowd.

Back down U.S. 23 to M-65; returning the country roads way.

Presque Isle County brings off a statistical surprise: eight percent of the nation's dark red kidney beans grow here. And a lot of potatoes. A conservative population of Polish, German, and Italian surnames keep the Catholic and Lutheran churches full and the farm produce piling up. Although beans grow in bigger volume, it's the potatoes that get their own festival on the first weekend after Labor Day. The festival is hosted by the 250 folks who live in and near Posen, a village so small it barely made it to the map.

But small never meant half-hearted. Posen's potato festival features oom-pah-pah music, polka dancing, and a mile-long parade watched by thousands, some of whom may have decided to stay around after the Labor Day Mackinac Bridge Walk (the only time you can hike across). There's a big potato smorgasbord, and 100-pound spud sacks can be bought for a song. Country action amid the first crimsons of fall.

M-65 goes quite a distance without reaching any towns, so mind the gas tank and your map. Then relax and watch for deer, forests, and meadows, sky-reflecting ponds and lakes. Take in the farms, trees, and changing skies of uninterrupted country. Chances to fish are everywhere; a world of wildflowers trims late-summer roadsides.

Maybe next time you'll come back with a snowmobile or cross-country skis. Or just as you are for another dose of the tranquilizing slowdown.

For More Information

Tawas Bay Tourist Bureau, 517-362-6281

Oscoda Lodging Association, 517-739-2021

Big Paw Resort, 517-724-6326

Alpena/Thunder Bay Regional Visitors Bureau, 517-354-4181

Cheyboygan Area Tourist Information, 616-627-2770

Rogers City Limestone Quarry, 517-734-2117

Gauthier and Spaulding Fishery, 517-734-3474

Hoeft State Park, 517-734-2543

Old Mill Creek State Historic Park, 616-436-7011

10

Roads to Hemingway's Michigan

Getting there: From Detroit, take I-75 north to Gaylord. Go west on M-32, north on U.S. 131 to Petoskey, then south on U.S. 31 to Walloon Lake.

Highlights: Hemingway hangouts, Horton Bay General Store, hunting, fishing, golf, skiing, and sailing.

". . . The woods ran down to the lake and across the bay. It was beautiful in the spring and summer, the bay blue and bright and usually whitecaps on the lake out beyond the point from the breeze blowing from Charlevoix and Lake Michigan."

> —Ernest Hemingway in "Up in Michigan"
> describing Horton Bay on Lake Charlevoix

Petoskey, Michigan, October, 1991: 125 people gathered in the tidy meeting rooms and mildly Victorian lobby of the historic Perry Hotel to read scholarly papers on a robust personality who made a life out of eschewing such gentility.

77

Traveling from as far as away as Switzerland and Japan (though most were from the United States), members of the Hemingway Society shared their mutual zeal for the works and world of Papa Hemingway. They steeped themselves in the boyhood vacationland of a fabulous talent, enjoying backcountry roads many Michiganians never get around to seeing.

Northern Michigan held a corner of Hemingway's soul. His first story, "Up in Michigan," was a natural. More fictional reflections of life here show up in "The Last Good Country" and "Indian Camp," the Nick Adams stories. Crisp morning mists, the tantalizing splash of a jumping fish, geese calling, wild game facing the barrel of his gun. The handsome youngster and youth, the greening writer who would win both Pulitzer and Nobel Prizes honed his senses and tested his mettle against real or imagined odds in these regions.

It certainly was nothing like Oak Park, Illinois, a suburb of Chicago where the Hemingway family lived. Ernest's father, a physician with allergy problems and an obsession for hunting, sought the pure air and outdoor freedoms of upper Michigan. In 1900 the family built a small cottage (later doubled in size) on the north side of Walloon Lake, between Charlevoix and Petoskey. Each summer parents and children boarded a steamer, puffed across Lake Michigan to Harbor Springs, entrained to Petoskey, then took whatever conveyance was available to the cottage.

Walloon Lake stretches long and narrow between green wooded hills toward Lake Michigan but doesn't quite touch the big pond. It is one of a string of lakes (Muskegon, Crystal, Torch, Charlevoix) just behind the Lake Michigan shoreline. Most of these smaller lakes have entries and exits to the big one, making for excellently sheltered harbors and ideal resort areas. Vacationing families from as far away as St. Louis populated the area's shores and inlets when Lake Huron's neighborhoods were still in quiet isolation.

Today, Walloon Lake and its surrounding square miles are thick with trees. However, the land and lake as Hemingway knew them had a different, barer look.

Long before tourists, lumbermen discovered the beauties of those slightly inland lakes. They made wonderful locations for mills. An "endless" source of timber on one side, easy shipping on the other, and insatiable markets just over every horizon. In the early 1800s the raid began. Nearly every town along the coast started with a sawmill. (There were over 2,000 mills in the state at one time.) The locusts of consumption went to work. In *Waiting for the Morning Train*, historian Bruce Catton (Pulitzer Prize winner from Petoskey) remembers the prairie landscape around Benzonia (in the same corner of the state) where today there are tall pines and hemlocks once again.

Joe Waldmeir of the Hemingway Society remembers how their treatises read, their research pondered, the visitors pored over E.H. memorabilia in the Petoskey Historical Museum (housed in the former depot): photos, books, and the Hemingway stamp dedicated in Montana, Key West, and Michigan on the same day.

They probably also hiked around town looking for haunts and survivors that only Hemingway buffs know about. Although a few dozen people a year come through the Petoskey Chamber of Commerce offices asking for Hemingway information, there is no printed guide to E.H. historic sites. (He would have done the legendary turn in his grave.) The Hemingway Society, however, knew him well. They knew life at the family cottage was not exactly a preview of the Brady Bunch, and that Ernest lived for a while in the house at 602 State Street, where he typed out his first short story. Real enthusiasts know about the Park Garden Café, where he used to play pool. (Beneath the wonderfully carved bar, a hidden tunnel led to a basement speakeasy.) No sign tells that Hemingway was here.

A bus trip down paths the author hiked led the group to the Hemingway cottage area on Walloon Lake. There is no name on the mailbox, but a few souls would recognize "Wildemere," the old family retreat. Ernest's favorite sibling, Sunny, lives in the house alone now. Perhaps embittered by the pressures of an intrusive public, the lady does not welcome visitors. No company. No interviews.

Next logical stop would be Horton Bay on Lake Charlevoix, a place for a boy like Ernest to hang around or run family errands. Later (after leaving and returning as a war hero), Ernest broke a couple of local hearts by marrying Hadley Richardson in a church that has long since burned down and been replaced. The village wasn't any bigger than it is now, so the Hemingways invited everybody in town to the wedding.

The old general store next door might sag a little more than it used to, but Ernest would be hard put to see any real changes. White frame with a false roof line, the relic wears a sign proclaiming HORTON BAY GENERAL STORE. GROCERIES—MEATS—BEER—WINE—ICE—FISHING TACKLE. About seven steps up to the front porch (where you can sit and rock) and a lot of Hemingway memories inside. Ask for Mr. Bill Ohle if you're a serious E.H. fan. He attended the wedding ceremony as a youngster.

U.S. 31, U.S. 131, M-66, and CR-48 form a circle around most of the bases for Hemingway searchers. Within this loop dozens of hilly backroads give you the feel of the country. They may be paved and posted, but deer can appear with startling speed at twilight, or a descendant of the quail Hemingway might have missed can be glimpsed disappearing into the grass. Mixed with summer estates are pioneer farm houses, old barns, and the remnants of fruit orchards or fresh plantings telling their own stories.

You can squint hard and imagine young Ernest taking his rifle, eager to shoot, enjoying the kill, bragging or lying about his deeds. He later said he believed this was part of his training as a writer. It is certainly part of anyone's discovery of the inner battles fought to appear courageous.

A maturing Hemingway ranged far wider to pursue game. He fished the Fox River in Michigan's upper peninsula and wrote about it in "Big Two Hearted River," a name better suited for fiction and one that wouldn't reveal where his favorite trout spot was.

Hemingway and Hadley never returned to Michigan after the honeymoon. The people who knew him then (and who weren't always pleased with what he wrote) have almost all gone on. Hunting and fishing still dominate north Michigan tavern conversation, only slightly ahead of golf or skiing. In time, such doings may produce their own storyteller, but not likely another Hemingway.

For More Information

Perry Hotel, 800-456-1917 or 616-347-2516

Petoskey Historical Museum, 616-347-2620

Petoskey Regional Chamber of Commerce, 616-347-4150

Charlevoix Area Visitor's Bureau, 616-547-2101

11

Tunnel of Trees

(M-119)

Getting there: Take I-75 north to Indian River, almost at the tip of the Michigan mitten. Take M-68 west to M-119, drive along the north side of Little Traverse Bay to Harbor Springs on Lake Michigan. This trip runs south to north.

Highlights: The lovely village of Harbor Springs, Good Hart Mission Village, Ottawa Indians, Cross Village, summer homes, woods and glimpses of the lake, beaches and dunes at Bliss Township Park.

In any random survey of favorite Michigan roads, the winding stretch of pavement between Harbor Springs and Cross Village will be mentioned. The person asked will probably want to stop the questions and tell about the last time he/she was on M-119, what season, what time of day. And they will refer to it as the "tunnel of trees," the best known nickname for any state road.

Running along the high embankment of upper Lake Michigan, M-119 is a slowpoke's dream. Anyone who even thinks about speeding through has the soul of Pac-Man.

The drive begins by turning west off U.S. 31 just north of Petoskey. M-119 passes Petoskey State Park along the north side of Little Traverse Bay in its short run to Harbor Springs, an enclave of prosperity, generations of gentility, and minds set against pop tourism. Part of any ride through the "tunnel" is a pause in Harbor Springs.

With a deep harbor-within-the-bay, Harbor Springs has been welcoming the grandest yachts on the Great Lakes for generations, playing the gracious hostess like a hardy dowager queen set in her role. Fine dining and select shopping are its draw-  ing cards, having successfully blocked the condos and fast-food outlets that have overtaken neighboring towns. Harbor Springs has a delightful time-warp feeling about it that makes browsing a holiday.

Years ago trains as well as steamers came here, but today the old depot is a boutique, and the strange six-sided house of Mr. Ephraim Shay (who invented a radical new locomotive in 1881) is filled with offices. You can step into the lobby for a glance at this eccentric building.

Holy Childhood Catholic Church, a wonderfully simple clapboard Gothic, looks toward mid-village, where new busi- nesses occupy vintage buildings as carefully tended as a cluster of Rolls-Royces.

The most exclusive enclave of "cottages" on all of Lake Michigan fills a long narrow peninsula separating the big lake from Little Traverse Bay. Here are summer retreats for such names as Ford, Libbey (glass), and Gamble (soap). You can't drive past their mutual gate, but another colony that you *can* drive past is on the east side waterfront. The Wequetonsing (WEE-kwee-TON-sing) area homes, real estate dreams, are visions of spaciousness, comfort, and grace.

Ottawa Indians had a large part in Harbor Springs his- tory before wealthy vacationers came, and nobody knows more on the subject than Veronica Medicine, outspoken curator of the Andrew Blackbird Museum. Blackbird, an Ottawa chief, founded the town's first post office, then became a writer and lecturer after being shoved out of this and other jobs. The museum on Main Street shouldn't be missed.

Following M-119 again to the top of a bluff, another row of old-family summer places surveys the scene and finds it good. Few houses ever seem to be on sale, but with the view they have of town, harbor, boats, and bay, that's easy to understand.

M-119 keeps to the edge up here. Around the first turn a friendly white farmhouse with green shutters and a red barn at its side welcomes guests as the Four Acres Bed & Breakfast.

Most of the open land seen along M-119 spreads out at this south end of the route. As the woods become thicker, the sun-surfaced lake sparkles between pines and birch as swiftly as a camera flash. There are houses all along the way but they are set back unobtrusively among the trees and range from simple to sumptuous. The Birchwood Inn, in a wide meadow, has motel annexes and a dining room; new posh houses can be seen in the Birchwood Estates development just up the road. A former schoolhouse, looking large enough to have been a two-roomer, seems now recycled into a private home.

When the woods close back around you, all distractions are melted by the sheer serenity of the road. Under a thickening canopy of green (or gold if you hit the color season), you move forward in soft curves, seldom far from the lake edge, to which the passage quickly returns. Always on a bluff, there are glimpses of rooftops, of houses standing at lake level on a very narrow strip of shore land. You may sense that you are going through a community, but hardly see it. This is a country road.

In winter, bare gray-black branches form a gothic aisle to altars forever around the next bend, and white ice on the lake can make the blue water seem even deeper. There is skiing in the vicinity during winter.

When the top of a church steeple appears among the treetops below the bluff, you've reached Good Hart, more of a
feeling than a village. The most visible commerce is an all-pur-
pose stop with two lethargic gas pumps, a post office, bakery,
real estate office, general store, and any other service the pro-
prietor can dream up. I bought a loaf of their special bread
made with Swiss cheese and rye flour; it was wonderful.

It was a December day and a Christmas tree stood blink-
ing in one corner; a 1910 brass cash register inherited from an
earlier store owner had just been polished to a high gleam.
Drawings of the church with the steeple rising to road level
were on the counter. His daughter did them.

A file for customer debts stood in a box on the counter; a
business pattern that matched the cash register. The super-
market generation will find this quaint.

Whoever you are and whatever you want to ask, the
owner is happy to oblige—about history, politics, or the ways
his neighbors live up to the town's name (which maybe should
have an "e" in the last half).

Next to the store a road runs downhill past a number of
shore homes and U-turns you back a mile to the tiny Indian
settlement of Mission Village, a living ghost town where three
hollow houses echo the wind amid new homes and the church
bearing the steeple. The whole of St. Ignatius Catholic Church
is a tall, classically simple white frame structure in good repair.
Founded by the Jesuits in the 1700s, it stands beside a large
cemetery filled with white wooden crosses, a tree-shaded resting place for many Indian citizens, a lot of them veterans of
American wars. During the summer months, mass is held on
Saturday evenings.

The "tunnel" goes on, teasing with quick views of Lake
Michigan and bending inland around large, tree-covered sand
hills that rise steeply against the road.

Then suddenly you're at Cross Village, where the curious stone building with stove legs across the roofline grabs everyone's attention. Things are even "curiouser" (to quote Alice) inside the Legs Inn.

Decades ago a Polish immigrant, Stanley Smolak, came to Michigan and started to build his restaurant-bar with whatever materials he could find. Gnarled and twisted logs, limbs, roots, and burls were adapted as table legs, balcony railings, archways, and whatever. Add huge stone fireplaces, excellent Polish-American food, and 20 kinds of imported beer and you've got a fun place with overtones of fairyland or a haven for gnomes. Legs Inn is now operated by Mr. Smolak's nephew, and is a recognized Michigan landmark. In warm weather, an outdoor dining area lets you gaze at the lake.

Here at Cross Village you can take a road across to I-75, but go on a little further on the county road extension. You won't get lost and the bluffs are left behind as you come to a stretch of sand dunes and beach called Bliss Township Park. Two outhouses render their necessary services, but beyond that, this is a rare, unspoiled beauty spot. This road, too, goes to Mackinaw City and I-75, or to the edges of Wilderness State Park, a grand, semi-wild acreage for nature lovers, campers, and backcountry bluffs.

For More Information

Andrew Blackbird Museum, 616-526-7731

Birchwood Inn, 800-530-9955 or 616-526-2151

Legs Inn, 616-526-2281

Wilderness State Park, 616-436-5381

12

Cruising the Eastern Woods

Getting there: Take U.S. 55 east or U.S. 23 to Tawas, where the routes meet, and head toward Grayling and Hartwick Pines. Or try the reverse route by starting from Hartwick Pines on M-93, just east of I-75 and two exits north of Grayling.

Highlights: Lumberman's Monument, legendary trout fishing and canoeing, last stand of virgin pine in lower Michigan (beautiful!) on self- or naturalist-guided tour, logging museums, Civilian Conservation Corps (ccc) bunkhouse and museum, small town attractions.

This is a trip for the trees. In a state with roughly 26,000 square miles of forest, nearly half of Michigan's total area, a suggestion to drive through the trees seems like telling a farmer to visit his fields. It's what we natives do all the time. Yet not being able to see the woods for the trees is one of our shortcomings. The country roads we now cruise belong to the Huron National forest, have fewer farms, offer more fishing sites than veggie stands, and teach a lot of history—natural and territorial.

Two hundred year ago Michigan was entirely forested. As the nation's population exploded westward in the 1800s, a consuming dragon was turned loose. Our trees were cut to rebuild Chicago and other cities after devastating fires. Trees became railroad ties, telegraph poles, ships, fuel, and more. By 1890 more than 700 logging camps and 2,000 sawmills in the state were cutting up to 3.5 billion feet of pine lumber each year. Much of Michigan became prairie while enormous fortunes were made by a squadron of lumber barons.

So complete was the logging that only three accessible stands of original timbers are left: Hartwick Pines (on this tour), Estivant Pines, and the Sylvania Recreation Area in the Upper Peninsula. Everything else is second or third growth.

For this country road adventure into the woods, start at the West Branch exit ramp off I-75 and take U.S. 55 east; or start at the Standish exit off I-75 and take U.S. 23 east and north. These routes meet in Tawas City at an intersection that offers food, gas, and nearby shelter. It's best to have a full tank.

Head north on Wilbur to Monument Road, through a woodsy residential neighborhood, past farms, and into the tree canopies of the Corsair Recreation Area. You may not want to go on. Miles of trails for hiking or cross-country skiing are maintained in the Corsair by the folks of Tawas; creeks and ponds for fishing can make you forget everything else.

Listen! A beautiful Michigan songbird called Kirkland's Warbler is recovering from near-extinction in these parts and can be heard if you're lucky. The fussy little creature wants only seedling pines in burned-over meadows for nest sites. Such odd habitat needs became scarce with modern fire controls.

Near the end of the road, the Kiwanis Memorial marks a tribute to the organization's gift of more than a million trees to one of Michigan's first reforesting efforts.

At the Au Sable River (Michigan's longest), an imposing piece of sculpture depicts three nine-foot bronze lumbermen holding the tools of their hardy trade. They are shown as serious fellows, with few clues to their real lives. The flesh and blood lumbermen, however, were probably a tad rougher look-ing. They had to cope with heat, cold, lice, a tedious diet, months away from home, low pay, hazardous conditions, no insurance or pension, and no goodies like bathtubs, washed flannels, or haircuts. They didn't write the policies of lumber-ing; they just worked like machines to get the job done. They earned their monument.

At the end of Monument Road are two other remem-brances. One is the United States Forest Service Monument on River Road toward Oscoda; the other is the Canoeists Memorial you'll pass going west on River Road to M-65. The annual two-person Canoe Marathon Race, covering the 120 miles from Grayling to Oscoda, is a major Au Sable event that is closely followed by paddleboat fans in late July. Watch for places to rent canoes up and down the river, and bring fishing rods. The scenic and meandering Au Sable has been a favorite brook trout stream, among its other virtues.

Take M-65 north through more corners of the Huron National Forest, Glennie, and the village of Curran; than go west on M-72, also known as Miller Road. (Depending on the season, you'll see masses of wildflowers, morel mush-room locales in the spring, and stunning color in the fall.) About five miles west of Fairview, M-72 takes a right turn south to Mio, but you continue straight on Miller until I-75. Travel north to M-93 (two exits up) and Hartwick Pines State Park.

The centerpiece of Hartwick Pines State Park is a beautiful 49-acre remnant of virgin forest. Standing in the middle like the regal queen she is, a tall pine called "The Monarch" remains a glory to behold, 150-feet tall, 45 inches in diameter, and more than 300 years old. Some of her long-gone relatives reached 200 feet and lived 500 years. Hard as you may crane your neck, the top is out of sight from ground zero.

Visit a reconstructed logging camp, a museum, and an interpretive center, and pose for pictures around the big wheels needed for pulling super-size timbers out of the woods. You can take a guided tour or explore by yourself on a well-marked path through the dark, wide trees. A small nondenominational log chapel makes a lovely resting spot on top of a midwoods knoll.

At 9,700 acres, Hartwick Pines, the largest state park in the Lower Peninsula, has much to tell about how a forest grows and falls, changes and adapts. Check the visitors center for maps and natural background material, then follow directions to the one-way, eight-mile Virgin Pines Scenic Drive. Signs will explain that you are seeing forests in various stages of growth and decay, and why bobcat and bear seek this kind of environment. After a mile or so, you cross over the east branch of the Au Sable River on a bridge that has seen better days, and into a large stand of straight and tall virgin jack pine. You pass a "mixed forest" next, with maples and tamarack, red pines, spruce, and hemlock. When bright sunlight filters though the trees . . . glorious!

Again the trail crosses the Au Sable, a clear bubbling flow, then moves into a red pine area that was planted by the Civilian Conservation Corps in the mid-1930s. Not a whole lot of sunlight reaches the forest floor here, discouraging new sprouts and therefore not appealing to browsing beasts.

Last to be described by a large sign is a maple grove where former trees have changed soil conditions and have been replaced by other trees, which are also eventually replaced. The final stand of maples in the cycle is called the "climax forest."

At the end of the trail you come again to M-93. A thick forest awaits up the road on the right (north); down the road to the left is the park entrance.

The park and campground are open all year, but exhibits run only from April to October, with limited hours in the spring and fall. A state park sticker is required. Of the 63 campsites, only 20 are without electricity.

If it is your choice to return to Tawas, try zigzagging a new way, going west to I-75 to bypass the National Guard artillery range, then east on Miller Road.

Those with an interest in the pre–World War II Civilian Conservation Corps may prefer a detour to see the CCC camp museum, which is 15 minutes south, near the northwest corner of North Higgins Lake State Park. Swing from I-75 to U.S. 27 and go left (east) on Grayling Road. A bunkhouse tells most of the story, which is that young men who lived and worked here planting trees had it only two slices better those who had chopped them down.

From this point, let impulses guide you to follow a new country road . . . through trees.

For More Information

Tawas City Chamber of Commerce, 800-55-TAWAS

Hartwick Pines State Park, 517-348-7068

Standish Chamber of Commerce, 517-846-7867

West Branch Chamber of Commerce, 517-345-2821

13

On the Back of a Sleeping Bear

Getting there: From I-75 at Gaylord turn west to Traverse City and continue on to Empire on M-72. Or travel north on U.S. 31 to Benzonia, take M-115 west to Frankfort, and go north on M-22 to Empire. The Sleeping Bear Dunes National Lakeshore visitors center is at M-72 and M-22.

Highlights: Scenery unmatched in mid-America, high dunes with accessible overlook platforms, appealing villages, historic light-houses; and heaven for bird-watchers and botanists.

First, the Ojibwe legend. A mother bear and her two cubs tried swimming across Lake Michigan to escape a Wisconsin fire. The mother made it but the exhausted cubs sank into the lake behind her. Unaware of her loss, the mother settled on a high shore bluff to watch for them, but fell asleep. The great spirit Manitou softened this tragedy by turning the cubs into nearby islands (North and South Manitou Islands) and the mother bear into a giant sand dune, close to her cubs forever.

A less poetic geologic history, however, presents a measured tale of advancing and receding glaciers that carved out the Great Lakes and left piles of debris along the edges. The Sleeping Bear National Lakeshore's dunes are "perched"; sand is piled atop cliffs that once stood nearly 600 feet high. The singular dune called Sleeping Bear is the most famous of these sand hills, although (like the others) wind has diffused some of its contours, reducing its height to less than 400 feet above the lake. It is thought to be the world's largest migrating dune, even though its movement makes glaciers look speedy. The 35-mile-long dune preserve near Traverse City will not easily blow away.

Within the lakeshore park's generous boundaries and its neighboring regions lies a network of country roads with sweet vistas. For prime sight-seeing, take Pierce Stocking Drive, 7.4 miles of pavement over the haunches of the Bear, winding between arches of beech and maple to panoramic views and glorious spots to picnic.

If you're traveling west from Traverse City via M-72, stop at the visitors center for pamphlets and a video presentation. Those coming north from Frankfort on M-22 and M-109 pause in Empire first and pack in some picnic meats from Deerings Market on Front (they have their own smokehouse). If there's time, browse through the Empire Area Historical Museum, an eclectic collection of the once-treasured, on M-22 at the LaCorea intersection. See old vehicles, a turkey feather Christmas tree, a model lumber mill, and even a fancy saloon bar. It's open every afternoon except Wednesday in mid-summer; other hours in the spring and fall.

Next, see the National Lakeshore Visitors Center. The drive entrance, just ahead off M-109, was named for Pierce Stocking, the lumberman who built this auto trail as an area attraction in the 1960s. A folder available near the entrance briefly explains what you are about to see. For the first half mile beyond the parking lot the road is a two-way drive, then a fork to the right takes you down a one-way path. Watch for walkers, bicyclists, motorcycles, and any urge to sneak above the 20 miles-per-hour speed limit.

The first stop is a high view of the Glen Lake vally and its beach and dunes. Not close enough for a swim, but the stop has picnic facilities close to a dune overlook platform. Lake Michigan and even the far Manitou Isles are part of the picture.

The next pause (if you want a good little hike) is the starting point for Cottonwood Trail, a 1.5-mile summit loop past buffaloberry and bearberry plants, which treads around "blowouts," bowl-shaped recesses scooped by the wind.

After this the road bends downhill through a stand of cottonwood trees, tough survivors in poor soil. You may feel like you're going in the wrong direction, but carry on. A big bonanza bluff-side lookout is the next-to-last suggested stop on the brochure. A large platform on the sand bluff affords airy views up and down the coast as far south as Point Betsie, the Manitous to the north, and perhaps some long ships passing on the west horizon. People on the beach hundreds of feet below seem startlingly small. The whole scene really stamps your brain cells when the sun is low over Lake Michigan, and gold light washes the sand, trees, and cliffs in surreal color.

The last suggested stop has more picnic tables where the view is south and west, and your tour is complete. At the exit, turn left on M-109 to the most popular sand pile in the state. With a large parking lot and summer concession stand, the Dune Climb hill, high and wide, is hard to resist. It looks easy, but climbing to the "top" will sop up any loose energy left in your youngsters. The reward is more of the same great views plus the dismaying discovery that the apparent top is only a plateau. There's more.

Continue north on M-109 to the place called Glen Haven, and make a left toward the Coast Guard Station Museum. The stretch of Lake Michigan between this mainland area and the islands is called the Manitou Passage. In the late 1800s and early 1900s dozens of ships came through daily with cargo headed for Leland, Traverse City, or Charlevoix. On a skipper's charts it would seem to be a time-saver compared to going out around the islands, but the channel was actually a dangerous route where shallow waters and hidden sandbars took heavy tolls. At the 1905 Life Station, crews stood ready to row to the rescure, even in freezing gales. A service boat, assorted gear, and photos of the selfless heroes are part of its exhibits today.

Arty, chic, warm, and friendly . . . a lot of things at once in Glen Arbor, a village captured and surrounded by the park. Small galleries and the Ken Scott Photography shop make Glen Arbor a growing magnet for creative minds and a fun place to browse through upscale sweaters, handcrafts, or the shelves of Steffens IGA to restock your larder.

For the camping crowd, the D. H. Day (near Glen Haven) and Platte River (south end of the park) campgrounds are open year-round on a first-come, first-served basis. There is water (not in winter) and vault toilets, but no hookups.

Upshore, Leland has a history of lumber, fishing, and summer visits by wealthy families. Between Lake Michigan and the oddly shaped Lake Leelanau, this is where you catch the ferry to South Manitou. A short stretch of river connects the two lakes and flows over the dam on its way out, bubbling through a photogenic little grouping called "Fishtown" (albeit most of the former fishing shacks sell candy or souvenirs to summer tourists). You can still buy fresh fish, too. It's in the National Historic Registry.

Leland's summer includes a festival waggishly named "Mona Leland Art on the Lawn Gala" in mid-July. The Leelanau Historical Museum has area history plus a display of ice shanty life artifacts, and Leland's cool shops specialize in original ideas.

In peak seasons reservations are needed to take the ferry to the Manitou Islands, both of which are part of the National

Lakeshore. No roads here, only country trails and traces of former streets. South Manitou, about nine square miles of exceeding pleasantness, rings with breezes in the treetops, bird calls, and lapping surf. The island was once a fuel (wood) supply dock for steamships, but few traces of old times remain. A handsome lighthouse and offshore shipwreck are points to observe, and you are given three hours to enjoy them unless you have a permit to camp overnight.

When visiting North Manitou, a designated wilderness, expect "a primitive experience, solitude, to use your self-reliance. For basic loners who relish a sense of isolation." On this, the much larger Manitou, 30 miles of well-marked trails make connecting loops. On both islands keeping track of time is vital if you don't have a permit to camp overnight. The visitors center provides updated infromation.

Return home, south or east, on back roads 677, 669, 651, and others. Enjoy fall-color eye feasts or spring delights when fruit blossoms are in full bloom. For country road fans who don't want to travel endlessly, the regions of the Sleeping Bear are ideal. Stop at the state travel centers (Clare, I-75) or local chambers of commerce for lists of accommodations and restaurants.

For More Information

Sleeping Bear Dunes National Lakeshore, 616-352-9611

Manitou Island Transit Information, 616-256-9061 or
   616-271-4217

Traverse City Visitors Bureau, 800-TRAVERS or 616-947-1120

14

Mackinac Island

Pedaling Around Camelot

Getting there: From Detroit, take I-75 north 285 miles to Mackinaw City and board the passenger ferry to Mackinac Island. No cars are allowed on the island.

Getting there: From the Upper Peninsula take I-75 to St. Ignace and board the ferry there. No cars are allowed on the island.

Highlights: The whole island is worth exploring by bicycle, horse and buggy, or on foot. Beaches, shipping on Lake Huron, Arch Rock, grand old houses, the Grand Hotel, and more.

No farms on this road. And no cars; only bikes and a rare buggy, although it is a full two lanes wide and paved all the way. Along the road's ample shoulders are goldenrod and wild asters, whitish stones tumbled to seductive smoothness by the lake, a limestone escarpment covered with trees, sailboats on the horizons. People nod as they pass.

Eight miles of country road in the spacious, carefree sense; a road to love for its general emptiness on the edge of Michigan's Mackinac Island. Locking both ends of the road together in a tender time warp, vintage hotels, shops, and houses zealously guard their 19th-century ambience.

Like a royal person set apart, Mackinac (MACK-in-awe) Island in northern Lake Huron presides over the Straits of Mackinac, passage to Lake Michigan. It is a bonbon of a place, wrapped in a sparkling foil of lore and legend where life looks as sweet as the fudge made in the Island village.

Even the approach is enchanting.

From the rail of a Mackinaw City (the only place spelling "Mackinac" with a "w"; always say "MACK-in-awe") ferry (Lower Peninsula), the island fits an Indian description: the back of a great turtle rising above Huron's crystal blue water. Soon the turtle image becomes a tree-covered dome with the handsome Grand Hotel anchored like a long white cruise ship among the greenery.

If you come from St. Ignace (Upper Peninsula), sumptuous "cottages" on a bluff are seen first. Posh real estate from another era. Ferries from both peninsulas dock in the Island's only harbor and village where inns and stores always wear fresh coats of paint. Boats bob in the marina, people are on bikes, and horse-drawn carriages clip-clop past. Cars are forbidden. A whitewashed fort on a cliff gleams in the background. Grass is greener than anywhere else, and the sun is dazzling on the flower beds.

If it were possible, I'm sure rain would be forbidden during daylight hours. Just like in Camelot.

Historic Mackinac served as our second national park (after Yellowstone), then was returned to Michigan. Today the Michigan State Parks own 82 percent of the island.

Visitors settle into quarters, take a carriage tour, and have lunch. The young and restless (or mature and healthy) who are done with general sight-seeing head for bike rentals. Singly or on tandems, they head to Lake Shore Boulevard. An island history pamphlet, a map (from the dockside visitors center), and a chunk of fudge for energy are all anyone needs.

Going east on Huron Street, pedalers pass Ste. Ann's Catholic Church, the oldest of the three island churches, then the Protestant Mission Church. Both have historic tales to tell if you stop and visit.

Just beyond the picket fences and shade trees of the village, the southeastern end of the island is dominated by the Mission Point Resort. The buildings once belonged to the Moral Re-armament movement, a peace-forever effort fostered after World War II. The structures now house hotel and conference facilities. Worth looking in on is the warm and lofty lobby, where a tremendous beamed ceiling resembles a sacred wigwam.

The road now opens up to the water, and if a ship is coming through, pull up a rock and sit down. It's a nice place to be when one of the stately ore freighters heading for (or coming from) Lake Superior goes silently through the channel between Mackinac and Bois Blanc Island. Nearly a thousand feet long, these are the unnatural successors to the splendid canoes of the Chippewas, who pulled ashore and held powwows or burials nearby.

Mackinac Island was discovered by Europeans in the 1600s. Fur trappers, French voyageurs, and Jesuit missionaries were here before Lake Michigan or southern Lake Huron was seen. It was claimed by the French, then ceded to the British, who built the island fort. The American Revolution gave Mackinac to the colonists, but it took the War of 1812 to settle ownership one final time.

The road bends northward, passes a private home with a gloriously lacy center gable, and edges beneath Arch Rock, a sizable limestone bridge. Riders can park their bikes and climb a path to get a better look at this rugged span.

Houses among the trees on the bluff don't interfere with the mood of solitude and serenity on the road. An "alone" feeling prevails even in August when all of the hundreds of island bikes are rented out.

The miles along a cliff can be windy as you roll toward one slight bend after another, thinking the next one will be the "top" of the island, and imagining buckskinned traders pulling up to camp or recount their furs before approaching one of John Jacob Astor's agents. Pelt buyers for Mr. Astor worked out of Mackinac Island warehouses (and made him the richest man in the United States) till the fur business dimmed and fleets of fishing boats came to dominate the economy.

Although the great freshwater lakes were a commercial fishing dream, an even bigger payload for the island was floating on the breeze.

As one garrison soldier wrote, "the air up here is so healthy you have to go somewhere else to die. . . . "

Poet and newsman William Cullen Bryant said, "the manifest fate of Mackinac to be a watering place . . . no air is more pure and elastic. . . . I cannot see how it is to escape this destiny." That was in 1846.

Others went further: "No better place for chlerotic girls and puny boys, worn out men and women suffering from overworked brain or muscle"; "bowel complaints seldom prevail"; "beneficial to those with nervous prostration."

Word like this got around. "Where asthma disappears!!"

Pedaling along you *do* feel as healthy as a new calf.

In the mid-1800s, an increasing traffic of affluent tourists, traveling on lake steamers with children, nannies, and personal maids came to board with residents for the season. Starting with a converted Protestant missionary society house, the hotel business went into gear.

Mackinac Island has belonged to the visiting public ever since, although it clings to its Victorian glory days the way a prom queen clings to her school years.

Finally, our road turns toward the west side and reaches British Landing, a rest area with motor-traffic amenities: rest rooms, refreshments, benches, and even a nature center.

Americans may have claimed Mackinac after the Revolution, but that didn't sit well with the British. During the War of 1812 they pulled off a successful raid (landing at this spot) and temporarily took everything back. Bikers can return to the village on British Landing Road, but it's an uphill ride.

On the last stretch of shoreline, the turrets and grand verandas of west bluff houses can't be seen. You see St. Ignace in the distance and the Mackinac Bridge; then suddenly back over your left shoulder rises the Grand Hotel, world's largest summer-only resort inn.

Grand Hotel

More than a hundred years ago the Grand was begun (with the help of big railroad money) in late summer and opened the following spring, even though winter supplies had to be hauled over the ice, and big sheets of plastic to cocoon the workers was unheard of. The opening was the gala event of the decade, with socialites from New York, Chicago, and Detroit in full regalia. The Grand has been associated with high style ever since. Today there's a modest charge for non-guests to stroll on the 660-foot three-story colonnaded front porch or to sit in one of the porch rockers, but they then enter select company: Cornelius Vanderbilt, Marshall Field, Mark Twain, Esther Williams, Steve Reeve, Jane Seymour (*Somewhere in Time* was filmed here), and presidents are among the VIP roster of catalog proportions. The porch fee includes the showcase gardens. No charge for standing at the driveway entry to photograph the rows of geraniums, the yellow awnings, or the antique carriages driven by coachmen in top hats and hunting pinks. A genteel, decorous life indeed (no shorts in the lobby).

Just beyond the Grand, the road rounds a turn, passes the venerable Windemere and Iroquois hotels, and meets the town center again. There are other roads lacing the island together, passing a school serving the 600 year-round residents, a Protestant and a Catholic cemetery, a landing strip for small planes, a golf course, the ruins of another fort, a strange tall rock called Sugar Loaf. Mackinac Island is a living, breathing place, not a museum. The shallow soil supports no agriculture, but there are wide varieties of flora and birds.

In winter, when horses have been transported back to mainland farms, the populace travels by snowmobile around the rim or on one of the cliff ridge foot trails. By January there is usually an ice bridge to St. Ignace, marked off with discarded Christmas trees.

Then spring again. Lake Shore Boulevard is free of ice; enough lilacs are budding to ensure a successful June festival. Put more paint on the porches, fire up the fudge kettles, check the bikes and rocking chairs. On Mackinac Island, great amounts of change are unlikely. Hooray.

For More Information

Mackinaw Area Tourist Bureau (for ferry information), 616-436-5664

St. Ignace Area Tourist Association, 906-643-8717

Mission Point Resort, 800-833-5583 or 906-847-3312

Grand Hotel, 906-847-3331 or 517-487-1800

15

To an Island in the Wind—
Drummond
(M-134)

Getting there: Take I-75 north to Mackinaw City (285 miles north of Detroit), cross to the Upper Peninsula on the Mackinac Bridge, and take M-134 east at exit 359. Follow M-134 around Lake Huron's northern shore to the Drummond Island ferry. Or, zigzag south from Sault Ste. Marie.

Highlights: Castle Rock, woods and water, Les Cheneaux Islands, ice fishing, hunting, fishing, skiing, antique boat show, wildlife, shipping in Lake Huron; an outdoorsman's paradise.

There aren't many choices. To reach the easternmost point in the Upper Peninsula, Drummond Island, you either zigzag south from Sault Ste. Marie, zip north or south on I-75 then turn east on M-134, or do your driving in a boat.

Coming north on I-75 means communing closely with the sky by driving across the Straits of Mackinac on the Mackinac Bridge (dimensions similar to the Golden Gate), stopping in St. Ignace for a fudge fix, and maybe getting high on Castle Rock, a chimney of limestone very close to the interstate.

The Castle has been climbed by generations of Michiganians. On a clear summer's day 25 pennies and many puffs of breath will get the physically fit to a blue-green wide-angle lookout over St. Martin Bay, St. Ignace, and Mackinac Island. The M-134 turnoff is too far up the road to see yet.

It's a little sad about promontory rocks. Although just getting to the top of the adjacent cliff gives a lot of pleasing visual mileage, American free enterprise has never wanted to leave accessible solitary high points alone. The Castle Rock business came before the new appreciation for leaving a unique natural form untouched. (Indians probably put a spirit up here and stood back.) But it's clean and well maintained. Kids (some with gray hair) linger over souvenir counters in the ticket office/shop or stare at the statues of Paul Bunyan wearing his plaid shirt and glazed expression (well, he had no fame as a wit) next to his blue ox, Babe.

Paul Bunyan statues are found in Wisconsin and Minnesota, too, but it was James MacGillivary from Oscoda, Michigan, who first collected folk yarns about an outsized logging Hulk Hogan.

Our goal road, M-134, skims the north rim of St. Martin Bay on northern Lake Huron, passing close to the mouth of the Pine River where a cluster of homes didn't quite gel into a town. The pines and cedars of the south edge of the Lake Superior State Forest (often so thick you might wonder how a deer could push through) are the whispering walls of this wide green slot to the east.

Half of Michigan is forest, but only by driving through these kingdoms of trees can you grasp the number of square miles involved.

It is the same with the Great Lakes, the magnificent blue expanses defining Michigan's boundaries, commerce, weather, mindset, and lifestyle. In the same way that the Alps mold the Swiss or the desert shapes the Bedouin, the lakes influence anyone within their draped contours. Michiganians are woods and water people.

When M-134 comes close to the shore, an urge to pull over comes on strong. Bays are rimmed with rock, sand, and pine, inviting waterside exploring—especially if the flies and no-see-ums of summer aren't stirring more than the wind.

This island-filled segment of Lake Huron's coast was the first corner of what is now Michigan to be seen by the Europeans. Squint south and picture the long canoes of Entienne Brule or Jean Nicolet, early French trappers, as they found their separate ways between the shoals of Les Cheneaux Islands, searching the dark trees for Indian campfires or river openings. Brule wanted furs; Nicolet hoped to find a shortcut to China. He was first to paddle into Lake Michigan and cross to Wisconsin. In his pack was an elaborate silk robe that he planned to wear to the emperor's court, but all he found were wild rice wetlands and puzzled natives. He didn't know he was the first white to travel the Great Lakes water route to the heart of a vast continent.

Campfires still burn, but electric lanterns, the glow of TV sets, and headlights extending vision over concrete trails in darkness tell of a different kind of world.

There are two communities on M-134 as it passes Les Cheneaux Islands: Hessel and Cedarville. Only three miles apart and with populations that dwindle to hard-core believers in the cold weather of winter, the two share events calendars and resort lists.

Les Cheneaux (LAY-she-NO; "the channels") are 36 wooded isles in 36 long and narrow sizes. They lie offshore at a southeast-to-northwest angle, as though they were being blown out to sea by a strong north wind. Most of them are privately owned.

Two miles before Hessel, Gordon and Annegret Goehring run Northwind Pottery, shaping up mugs, bowls, and dinnerware out of local clay and natural themes. If their little shop on the north side of the road isn't open, call and make a date to stop in and chat with this well-informed, history-minded couple.

You can tour Hessel in ten minutes, maybe less. Tiny and neat, a gazebo in Marina Park adds a quaint touch to the big Antique Boat Show and Art Fair in August. There is a general store and a couple of places to eat, some very old buildings, and bright new dwellings. Ask what they do in deep snow seasons and citizens just go blank. How do you explain ice fishing to a hothouse stranger from Detroit? Snowmobile, cross-country ski, go up to the Indian casino near Sault Ste. Marie and play a few rounds.

Cedarville looms a few tads larger than Hessel. The big business of both villages consists of lumberyards and limestone shipping, and making visitors happy: finding them cabins and resorts, docking boats, supplying fishing and hunting gear, ferrying people to islands, and cooking them dinner.

There's a neat historical museum in Cedarville that sponsors the big joint-community event of the year, the annual Antique Boat Show in Hessel on the second weekend in August.

This is the show that could and did. From a modest start, it has become the largest of its kind anywhere, bringing together old dinghies, canoes, steam launches, power cruisers, classic sailboats, and anything built before the days of fiberglass—pleasure and workboats on which tender care and considerable amounts of money have been lavished.

Poke through the Woodshed Gift Shop, a Victorian emporium for handcrafted baskets, paintings, rugs, antiques, and more. Hours vary, so call. It's half a block south of the M-12 and M-134 intersection.

Just east, a south side driveway into the limestone operation doesn't forbid entering, but it's not a tourist attraction. I
suggest driving in a few yards, just far enough to see the long
freighters at anchor or waiting their turn at the loader.

There's another long and wonderful swoop along the coast
and a scenic turnout for views unblocked by islands just before
DeTour Village. The term "gateway to" is badly overused by
any town that wants you to go through their portals to reach
anywhere else. However, DeTour is a true gate, opening into
the St. Mary's River and thence to Lake Superior. The name
means "the turn," and this was a community when Chicago
was still a swamp, Detroit an empty opening on a bluff. As the
main bend on a water highway, this spot has had a navigation
light since 1848; the light you see offshore was built in 1931.

The brochures on DeTour, a town just eight blocks long
and three to five blocks wide, list eight or nine places to eat
and/or drink, a couple of motels, and five churches. Some of
the listed are actually in Goetzville, 14 miles away.

I had breakfast in the Pointe DeTour Café. Blue-checked
vinyl on the tables, curtains at the windows, and good-soup
hominess. Neighbors came in, sat down at the same long table,
and with an occasional glance my way, put on a U.P.-type talk
show, rambling softly about outboard motors, weather, rifles,
and didjaknows. I felt like joining in.

DeTour is a choice town for freighter-watchers or anyone
who might want to charter a boat and chase those Atlantic
salmon now thriving in the St. Mary's River.

M-134 loops to an end here, but natural extensions are the
roads of Drummond Island, a woodsy destination rising on
the charts.

A ferry big enough for two dozen autos (if there aren't
too many long RVs on board) shuttles to the island most of

the year. You can see Drummond's lone industrial plant, a limestone operation, from across the water and in minutes you're going between the tall blockhouses with an overhead connection—the archway saying WELCOME TO DRUMMOND ISLAND: GEM OF THE HURON.

Drummond is the largest of the U.S. Great Lakes islands, of an indefinable shape but built to a northern outdoor person's specifications: lots of forested campsites, good hunting and fishing, and 150 miles of shore where cliffs, coves, harbors, and simple notches in the rocks give every mile its own profile. Once this place was British territory, and even had a fort named for Sir Gordon Drummond. After the War of 1812 it was U.S. property, although the British commander at that time was slow to believe this bad news and kept adding to the fort. The few traces that remain of this era are on private property.

Eighty miles of paved roads and endless trails curl around wetlands and through trees, past wild strawberry patches, raspberries, and a botanist's delight of wildflowers. Of the 54 known species of orchids native to Michigan (some of them minuscule wonders), 24 can be found here. In the windswept forests of spring, searchers hunt coveted morel mushrooms and the edible greens of delicate fiddlehead ferns.

Over 200 species of bird flit before the patient observant eye, from purple finches and scarlet tanagers to bald eagles, owls, and cranes.

Half of Drummond is state-owned, but visitors must be careful about hiking across someone's back forty. There is a village, a "downtown" called Four Corners, and gathering places for natives and strangers. Creature comforts like fresh crullers or apple pies, fishing supplies, swift meals, and those tourist staples, souvenir T-shirts, are easy to find. You can bowl if the urge hits or play golf on two courses. One of them has an unusual hazard—an airport landing strip that crosses its fairways. I wondered if pilots put their heads out and yell "Fore!" before landing.

Drummond Island, nature haven, is a civilized place.

For More Information

St. Ignace Area Tourist Association, 906-643-8717

Northwind Pottery, 906-647-3416

Woodshed Gift Shop, 906-484-3002

Drummond Island Chamber of Commerce, 906-493-5245

Upper Peninsula Travel and Recreation Association, 906-774-5480

16

Along the North Rim

(H-58)

Getting there: On the Upper Peninsula, east to west. From St. Ignace just across the Mackinac Bridge, take U.S. 2 west along Lake Michigan's north shore. Turn north on M-117 to M-123 just below Newberry. North of Newberry, H-58 circles westerly to Munising.

Highlights: Pictured Rocks National Lakeshore, Taquamenon Falls, swimming, hiking, fishing, birding, wildlife, Grand Marais, Grand Sable Dunes.

Dented by few inlets and seemingly untouched by commerce, great lengths of Michigan's north coast stand high above Lake Superior. Like a fortress against the sea, unyielding cliffs are battered by rams of ice and storm and the pressures of unblocked winds. They not only remain firm but are havens of serenity and peace.

This is the shore of Gitchee Gumee, shining big-sea water, of murmuring pine and the hemlock so enthralling to poets, naturalists, hikers, rockhounds, campers, fishermen, and anyone who isn't a thoroughbred couch egg.

Too impressive to be dallied with, one such stretch between Grand Marais and Munising has become Pictured

Rocks National Lakeshore. Less dramatic but still enchanting is the forested coast eastward to the tiny community of Deer Park. Using backcountry roads H-58 and CR-407 part of the way, you can access the national park and skirt the north shore. It's a good wide road, mostly gravel with strong proclivities to washboarding and dust, but easy to follow. Roads near the coast *east* of Deer Park may need four-wheel drive.

By the time you get to Perch Lake, where H-58 heads west from CR-407 and H-37, the dedicated wanderer has seen a lot. Taquamenon Falls, one of the largest spills (after Niagara) east of the Mississippi, is not far away. Persons who come this far should have seen freighters going through Sault Ste. Marie locks (the "Soo" Locks) and hunkered over artifacts of the *Edmund Fitzgerald* (a sinking made famous by a Gordon Lightfoot song) in the Whitefish Point Marine Museum.

Driving up from Newberry through the mixed birches and evergreens of a second-growth forest, a name familiar to Hemingway fans will flash past. The road crosses the "Big Two Hearted River," scene of a sighing tale. Scenic and inviting, the view from the low bridge has photographic charms, but this is not the real river of the story. Hemingway fished in the Little Fox then shrewdly protected his spot by writing of a river with a more theatrical name.

At Perch Lake H-58 angles off to the left, but I like to continue to Deer Park on Lake Superior and Muskallonge Lake State Park, where you find a trio of resorts and not much else. A real town once stood on the narrow strip between the two lakes, whirring with a sawmill, a hotel for company, and a store for spending. If the hotel lacked a saloon, there was probably one of those as well. That bygone lumbering life has been replaced by 179 modern campsites along Muskallonge's shores within yards of Lake Superior. Lake Muskallonge is shallow enough to warm up a mite by August, making it pretty good for swimming compared to the liquid freeze of Superior.

Some 71,000 visitors manage to arrive annually, filling campgrounds in summer, yet leaving a wondrous spaciousness. Wear pockets to Lake Superior beaches for little agate treasures or colorful bits of granite; search the spring woods for mushrooms along miles of trails. Sometimes the flies go slightly mad and the no-see-ums fly through screening two abreast, but with any wind at all and some good anti-bug juice these pests can be minimal.

CR-407 twists and turns, finally meeting H-58 again to follow a serpentine trail to Grand Marais. There are frequent old logging paths to the water's edge, most of them warning you back with wide shimmering puddles.

The forest is a place to learn and observe; nature guides should be to glove compartments what spare change is to wallets. Aside from a specimen of every kind of northern tree in the book, hawks and barred owls, woodpeckers, porcupines, foxes, bobcats, and bears (all elusive creatures) call this home. Sometimes you'll spot the long scratch marks of a black bear on a tree trunk, but I've never met one on this road.

The road curves on . . . and on . . . and on. Curling miles always seem longer than straight ones.

If there is ever a contest for ugly names in a pretty place, a few votes would go for Blind Sucker River, Dead Sucker River, and Blind Sucker Flooding, water sources for two popular fishing and state forest camping sites off H-58 near a third campsite on Lake Superior. It may be cozy among the trees of the two inland sites, but Superior shoreline campers cope with cool, chilly, and cold. "Warm" is a lucky afternoon bonus. Follow a tested practice: keep tent flaps and trailer doors facing the woods rather than the lake, remembering how the wind coming across a frigid surface wants to warm up on your hide.

"Grand Marais, voilà!" is probably what the first French voyageurs said when they paddled into this pretty little harbor seeking canoe refuge from Lake Superior storms. A lighthouse, park, dock, a few cottages and stores—Grand Marais makes you want to set up an easel and paint.

Too small for today's freighters, in its heyday the town was a big lumber-shipping center with wild and wanton ways. Thirty saloons, a dozen hotels and boarding houses, two newspapers, the Alger-Smith sawmill, and a train to Marquette kept the money circulating. Now the village has rooms for 250 travelers and a steady population of 500, mostly determined not to let developers alter the ambience.

Best treat in town is a stop at the Earl of Sandwich Shop, standing with its back to the harbor in the center of a one-block downtown. Fresh-made ice cream hand-dipped into waffle cones. Forget restraint.

From the west side Woodland Township Park (modern campsites, tennis courts, playground) you can hike along the beach to the base of the Grand Sable Dunes. As the teen set would say, "Totally awesome." The dunes form the eastern end of Pictured Rocks National Lakeshore and should be seen from lake level looking up to appreciate their impact on the first European explorers who saw and wrote excited descriptions: "massive hills of sand whereupon a man standing seemed no bigger than a crow . . . "

They are "perched" dunes, piles of gravel pushed aside by the glaciers that bulldozed the lake bed, then buried under tons of sand. Slanting upward from the beach at 35 degrees (maximum angle for sand to "hold" before it avalanches downward), the long embankment rises to heights of 275 feet. On top are five square miles of shifting sands and dunes like 80-foot waves cresting on a tawny sea.

Because of the pitch, climbing up the face of these dunes is extremely risky; better to use H-58 access points to reach the top. Such a chance comes up at a bend in the road and the turnoff to Sable Falls. Tucked behind the easternmost sand hills, a trail forks one way to the high sand; the other way steps down into a tree-sheltered gorge beside the delightful falls. Follow the first fork far enough (it gets strenuous), and you come to a magnificent view of Lake Superior. The trail to the cascade follows Sable Creek around to its outlet and you are on the beach again.

At the visitors center, next stop west, you can pick up maps, histories, and instructions, and have questions answered.

The pavement is gone for a while; back to gravel. Unless it starts pouring rain or you are in a deep fog (unlikely), detour up to the Log Slide, walk a wooden trail to two overlook platforms, and enjoy a view unmatched in the Midwest. Eastward you are looking at the long profile of dunes as they face the inland sea; westward to the low and forested Au Sable Point with its lighthouse visible above the trees. Late in the 19th century the Log Slide site was a stream of tumbling tree trunks as lumberjacks cleared the forests behind them, the only invasion this coast ever knew.

A long hiking trail along the rim of the park coast cuts near the platforms making a good entry point. A little farther, Hurricane River Campground has all the facilities and another trail contact, the closest route for anyone wanting to check out the lighthouse. The sturdy red brick structure is a fine example of lighthouse architecture, built in 1874 and listed in the National Register of Historic Places. You are invited to climb to the top.

H-58 has more treats with a difference. If you are lucky, bright sunlight will be sending shafts of radiance through the green or yellow leaves and massed white trunks of the park's spreading white birch forest. It is hard not to become a little rapturous amid a scene as stunning as any in all of nature. When winter strips the trees to their basic forms, another kind of beauty in black and white dazzles the beholder. There is no off-season for such a place.

Ambling south, H-58 goes away from the perimeter of the park, deeper into Lake Superior State Forest, past burned and cut areas, meadows, maturing second growth, and the haunting sounds of silence . . . if you stop the car and listen. Side roads (more old logging trails) lead south to camping and fishing sites; north to the shore.

At Van Meer, however, where H-15 heads down to Shingleton, the Bear Trap Inn and Bar whips up a pleasant break for camping cooks with steak, lobster, fresh fish, and homemade pies. No overnights at this inn; just friendly types to swap tales with.

Miner's Castle Road leads to a towerlike rock formation jutting from shore—the only good place to see what this "pictured rocks" business is all about without going for a boat ride. It's high above the water but safety engineered with fences and handicap ramps. One short detour goes to Miner's Falls, another to the beach.

The west end visitors center stays open all year (actual park headquarters sits on a coast road), a boon to snowmobilers and cross-country skiers.

Munising is said to be the Ojibwa campsite where "daughter of the moon, Nokomis" cared for little Hiawatha. On a clear blue bay and tucked into a horseshoe of green hills spilling with waterfalls, the town is county seat, travel center, diving destination, and port for boats that will take you on a cruise to see the Pictured Rocks in their full glory.

Strewn around the harbor depths and along the coast are rocks, caves, and half a dozen sunken ships that make up the attractions of the Alger Underwater Preserve. Some of the ships are virtually intact, others are scattered in bits and pieces, but the cold fresh water does little damage to these relics. (However, a new marine menace, the zebra mussel, has the potential to ruin everything.)

The large island you see near the harbor has been acquired by the state park department and is headed for very cautious development.

From the Pictured Rocks cruisers, the coast story becomes complete. Towering limestone walls continue for miles and ooze with surprising color. Pocked with caves, arches, and twisted formations, the vertical showpieces plunge into the water with no ledge or beach. Any storm-tossed sailing ship or canoe would view these walls with terror, but we can gaze safely at the random arts of nature; see the works of eroding waves.

Munising has charter boats, diving equipment rentals, and a fair supply of motels and restaurants. Cuisine tends toward simple and hearty; this is not an enclave of sophistication.

Looping back to the east on M-28, stay alert. For 25 miles this highway runs straight enough to set your ruler by—which tends to get boring. Just south, the Seney National Wildlife Refuge, large enough to be its own county, offers birdwatching spots and hikes along marked paths. No driving around on your own, but a schedule of auto safaris takes visitors to where the bears might be. The entrance is on M-77.

Another kind of wildlife lies peacefully buried on Seney's "Boot Hill," a Tombstone, Arizona, sort of place. The tiny Seney Historical Museum may be able to tell you more . . . if it's open. Otherwise, settle for coffee at the gas station, often the best stop for filling up on local history.

For More Information

Information on The Great Lakes Shipwreck Historical Museum at Whitefish Point available through 906-635-1742 (Great Lakes Shipwreck Society, Sault Ste. Marie)

Taquamenon Falls State Park, 906-492-3415

Muskallonge Lake State Park, 906-658-3338

Lake Superior National Lakeshore, 906-387-3700

Upper Peninsula Travel and Recreation Association, 906-774-5488

17

Brockway Mountain Drive—
Step Out into the Sky

Getting there: Leave M-26 just west of Copper Harbor and rejoin it 10 miles later.

Highlights: Panoramic views of Lake Superior, uncommon floral species, Mount Houghton, Eagle Harbor.

Although U. S. 41 can take you to the tip of Michigan, Brockway Mountain Drive actually lets you rise above it. Take a ride on Brockway, the highest pavement between the Alleghenies and the Rockies.

Brockway's lofty detour leaves M-26 just west of Copper Harbor then rejoins it 10 miles later, five miles from Eagle Harbor. Taking this east-to-west approach, much of the trip to the top is a fairly steep, low gear, have-faith-in-your-car affair. Especially the first quarter mile.

For first-timers, getting out at the second hairpin turn has the makings of a law. Those who don't stop miss Brockway's first gift to the senses, a panoramic view of Lake Superior, Copper Harbor, town and inlet, Lake Fanny Hooe and the hills beyond, the lighthouse on its little point of land, and the flagpole at Fort Wilkins.

One can imagine Chippewas here, beseeching the hovering spirits or wondering about those who come in canoes with white wings and no paddles.

From this nearly hallowed bluff I have watched the early grays of dawn give way to orange sunrises then rheostat up to full daylight, changing dark hills from sleeping animal shapes to their forested realities with amazing speed. A balcony seat for the quiet drama of a northern morning but lovely any time of day.

The road edges the south rim of the Brockway Mountain, a path into un-Michigan-like space. Birch, sumac, and scrub pine have managed to survive on the thin soil cover of this stone hill, part of the Precambrian shield, and among the oldest surface rocks on the planet. Brockway's layered sediments have been pushed into a sharply titled stance, like a thick slab of cement when the sand under one end vanishes. Here and there a low stone wall serves to reassure the skittish.

Rising, dipping, rising again, dipping again, turning and twisting its way higher and higher, the road tempts only the simpleminded to rev it up. Too much to enjoy; too many blind curves.

Several times the summit seems just ahead, but false alarms are the road's own game. What you *do* see are forests across a small valley, outsize blackbirds perching on the wall then vanishing with a swoop to unseen goals below. In some seasons there are dozens of migrating hawks riding the updrafts along the cliffs; sometime you may see an eagle.

The semi-alpine ecosystem near the top is a botanist's delight, where floral species found nowhere else in the state find a refuge. Orchids (some incredibly tiny), trillium, harebell, and thimbleberries sometimes require diligent searching, but they are here.

One last uphill surge and the goal is reached: a windy aerie for earthlings.

There is no grander vista in Michigan. On the north side Lake Superior stretches out 600 feet below, vast and blue—the largest, deepest, and coldest of the Great Lakes. On a clear day the faint shadow of Isle Royale National Park hovers off to the northwest. There will probably be a freighter or two on the horizon, heading to or from Duluth, Minnesota, or Thunder Bay, Ontario. This is a few counts down from six or seven long ships visible from Brockway Mountain when the iron ranges of Minnesota's Masabi Range were in top production. Today's ships carry taconite (iron pellets) and wheat from the American/Canadian Midwest.

The summit can be driven around, but not to get out is to sail and stay below deck. Brockway requires walking the small circle, feeling the wind (which can get colder than a polar bear's heart in late fall), and smelling the total freshness.

Your eye will trace the trees to the inlet town of Eagle Harbor beyond Lake Bailey. A tiny island gives the roundish lake a doughnut look, even as it glimmers flatly in the sun. There are hills to the west in line with Brockway but right in line and part of the same formation. Sloping up, then dropping abruptly off, they resemble waves frozen before the moment of white cap. The top of the crest nearest to Brockway Mountain is reached by a long hiking trail, a marvelous place to pick blueberries in August.

Keep turning. Other hills seem rounder, less dramatic. Mount Houghton, highest rise in the Keweenaw Peninsula, stands on the other side of the peninsula. Filling part of the hollow between, Lake Medora, holding a satisfying supply of bass and pike, is scenic and never crowded, with a public access site off U.S. 41.

Facing straight south now, Brockway breaks off abruptly over the forest. No roads or paths down there, just pines and birch and a few hardwood—a gold-splattered vision in autumn. A curving dent shows where a brook should be running, but only melting spring snows can make it flow.

The opening in the next slope of trees belongs to the Keweenaw golf course; east of that lies Lake Fanny Hooe. Trees keep this from being a full-circle view, but you are quickly back to staring out over Lake Superior. On some days clouds make it impossible to see anything past the large descriptive sign.

In the summit gift shop, copper country books, cards and pictures, and all the trinkets dear to tourist hearts are available, plus refuge from the wind.

Going downhill toward Eagle Harbor is not nearly the same twisting experience that coming up was. Delightful and straight, the drive ends near Silver Creek Falls. At the nearby "Jam Pot" two friars bake wondrously fine bread and rolls and put up thimbleberry or blackberry jam to support their religious efforts.

The coast drive from here west and around back to U.S. 41 will take you past sand dunes and "agate" beaches (if you know exactly what you're looking for), then to Eagle River, Keweenaw County Seat.

18

The Last Lap North

(U.S. 41)

Getting there: From Chicago, take I-94 and I-43 north through Wisconsin to Menominee, Michigan, in the Upper Peninsula. Drive U.S. 41 north from Menominee. The trip runs south to north.

Getting there: From Detroit, drive I-75 north to the Upper Peninsula. At St. Ignace, take U.S. 2 west 130 miles along the northern shore of Lake Michigan to U.S. 41 at Rapid River. The trip runs south to north.

Highlights: Investigate Copper Country, pasties, the ghost town at Fayette, Laughing Whitefish Falls, and Marquette; skiing, moose, birding in Keweenaw Bay, a Finnish community in Hancock; Calumet and Copper Harbor, Fort Wilkins, and Brockway Mountain Drive.

At one end of the road, Florida sunshine, citrus groves, glamour spas and houses built to catch every breeze. Tampa, Fort Myers, and soft warm sands not far from a great wild place with alligators, egrets, and moss hanging from cypress like shredded drapery. Then Miami. Megalopolis cityscape; sprawling, savvy, rich, and desperate, where magnetic rhythms, styles, age, and accents clash or meld in uncertain intimacy under a glazing sun.

Far away at the other end of the highway, Michigan towns with houses built for warmth; resorts where glamour keeps a low profile and cozy wins over chic. Vast tracts of pine, tamarack, cedar, and birch, sheltering creatures with thick fur and snow wisdom. On into Copper Country. Less than 25,000 people in the two counties of a rocky peninsula poking into icy Lake Superior. Ghost towns and old mines. In the last tiny village the sweet slow pace is as plodding as a black bear's amble and the sky is likely to be cloudy.

Between these extremes, U.S. 41 was once a north-south "Route 66," the paved rope tying Houghton, Marquette, and other Michigan points to Milwaukee, Chicago, Nashville, and the tantalizing allure of Florida. The pre-interstate snowbird connection: U.S. 41 south to the sun or north to escape the heat.

After big cities, commotion, wide rivers, a drift of mountains, and sometimes expansion to four lanes, the Michigan portion of U.S. 41 is a quieting down. Small cities amid miles of forest. Only tiny segments of double lanes. A sometimes disquieting amount of uniformity.

In Michigan, this is a country road that enters the state at Menominee (the name means "wild rice" and this is a good place to buy it) from Marinette, Wisconsin. The two towns are pals and rivals on the banks of the Menominee River as it flows into Green Bay (Lake Michigan).

In early 1600, French voyageur Jean Nicolet put his canoe ashore near Menominee carrying an incredible bundle under his arm. Nicolet, first European to venture westward across Lake Michigan, hoped to find China on the far side. (He also thought the lake would become salty.) The bundle was an elaborately embroidered silk robe to wear when meeting the emperor. Instead he met only rightfully puzzled Indians; the vast land expanses of the continent were still a secret.

Nicolet, however, broke a time barrier. After him came the trappers, missionaries, and settlers; the white invasion. Tall and silent forests were seen by this new breed as a field to be harvested. Menominee's river floated a staggering five million feet in tree trunks in 1893, making the town the lumbering capital of the world until the supply ran short.

The forest has returned (without the super-sized white pine, Michigan's state tree) and is the main roadside attraction as our highway continues north. No beeline path, there is a wide swing to the east through Escanaba and then up to Marquette, largest city in the Upper Peninsula . . . which at 25,000 inhabitants will strike some readers as humble. Both cities have points of interest and every fast food you can name.

A local specialty that U.P. visitors have *got* to try is a pasty (rhymes with *nasty*), a hefty meat pie that's been a lunch staple for generations of miners. They can be dry and crusty, but a good pasty hangs in the memory like Mom's fried cakes. While you're pumping gas, ask where the best pasties are and head for that eatery.

Escanaba ("Eskie"), half the size of Marquette, likes to call itself the "Riviera of the North." Well, leave your bikini in the suitcase. The waters of Little Bay de Noc (part of Green Bay on the northwestern side of Lake Michigan) seldom rise above cold. Natives handle it but few others can. There's a great wide waterfront park, however, with summer band concerts and a lighthouse museum, and the cozy old Ludington House Hotel. Amid brass fixtures and lace curtains, the Ludington has lunch and dinner waiting.

North of Escanaba, U.S. 41 turns at Rapid River, but if time is no problem, I suggest a detour. Follow U.S. 2 east of Garden Corners, then M-183 south to Fayette Historic State Park (about 50 miles altogether). You'll pass some of the best farms in the north, a hamlet called Garden, and finally come to the state park and Fayette, prettiest ghost town anywhere.

This delightful haunt occupies a site straight out of a movie set. High limestone cliffs in the background of a tiny snail-shaped harbor; blue-blue water, thick green pines, and the gray buildings of the town, thoughtfully preserved in their dull weathered state instead of being brought back to an artsy newness with fresh paint. A fragmented foundry and charcoal kilns tell of a company town smelting ore into pig iron. That was between 1867 and 1891.

Fayette's opera house, boarding house, blacksmith's, doctor's office, and worker's residences are on the self-guided tour. A handsome visitors center has an exceptionally large-scale model of the town giving more details, while showcase exhibits fill in with mineralogy, geology, and local history.

The state park has campsites (but no food) available, and some nice hikes to the top of the cliff.

Back on U.S. 41, the drive to Marquette cuts across state and national forest areas, through a spruce and pine kingdom where occasional rivers tempt fishing fans to pull out their gear. For a waterfall refreshment hour, detour east to Sundell (between Dukes and Rumely) on M-94, then north on the paved road. When it becomes dirt, turn right at the first wide intersection and follow to a parking turnabout. Walk half a mile through birches and northern hemlock, down some steep steps, and you're at the base of Laughing Whitefish Falls, a noisy, buoyant cascade pouring 70 or 80 feet into a deep gorge. In spring, it's a torrent of delight. You will be impressed. (There are more than 150 waterfalls in Michigan's Upper Peninsula.)

U.S. 41 gives a first glimpse of Lake Superior while entering the rocky hill city of Marquette. Our highway would have you

Fayette

bypass the downtown area of this sturdy civic establishment and "shopping center of the U.P.," so don't take the turn west under the viaduct but keep going up Front Street and browse through town. Lumbering and a great lode of iron ore have been off/on staples of the area economy for over 150 years.

In the red stone and newly restored Marquette County Courthouse, Lee Remick, Ben Gazzara, and Jimmy Stewart played their memorable roles in *Anatomy of a Murder*, written by the late Marquette lawyer, judge, author, and foremost U.P. fly fisherman, John Voelker, alias Robert Traver.

A visitors center on Front Street will point you to other highlights: the campus of Northern Michigan University (and maybe a play or concert), the winter Olympic training center and world's largest wooden geodesic dome arena, and a working dock still loading long freighters near Presque Isle Park. Or try a sightseeing cruise from the waterfront.

You don't get back to "countryside" immediately, but soon. First, U.S. 41 zips past Negaunee and Ishpeming, towns steeped in iron-mining tradition—with a dandy new museum to tell you all about it. But there is something else to note: the discovery of iron and copper in the Upper Peninsula brought hordes of immigrant miners from Europe, including the Norwegians and Swedes (whose names still dominate Marquette area phone books). Those hardy types with homemade skis had a heavy influence on the sport, as seen in the National Ski Hall of Fame on U.S. 41. They'll give directions to "Suicide Hill" where ski jumping and hot-dogging caught on.

By now you may have heard that native-born Upper Peninsulites are called "Yupers," with an accent all their own and a hearty sense of informal humor. "Da Yoopers," an off-the-charts singing group filling time on local radio stations, belts out lyrics about deer camp saunas or fishing for Moby Dick in a pontoon boat. The group's tunes are available on tape for home or car listening (just for fun).

Great expanses of forest worry some people with fears of bears and lesser creatures. The Oz message, "Lions and tigers and bears, oh my!" doesn't help, despite the truth that bears are shy, nocturnal, and can usually be frightened off with a loud voice. Do not approach for close-up photos, however.

Today's black bear has a new competitor for attention. Moose were reintroduced into this area of northern Michigan a few years ago and are doing pretty well. MOOSE CROSSING signs to the contrary, the chances of seeing one along the highway are slim; moose are solitary, backwoods creatures who love the vegetation of shallow lakes. However, you might *hear* one at lunch across a lake—a single moose slurping up water weeds sounds worse than three plumbers with plungers on the same drain. As with bears, forget getting close to a moody moose.

On Lake Michigamme, Van Riper State Park (moose info center) offers tent and trailer space, while the slightly pricey Michigamme Lodge lures bed-and-breakfast fans with luxury and style. The two-story log lodge, built by a successful Russian immigrant merchant, has a historic plaque and its own gift shop.

U.S. 41 turns north and passes the trail to Sturgeon River Falls (another deep-woods treat if you have the time) and Alberta, a Michigan Technological University Forestry station. Alberta belonged to the Ford Motor Company back in the days when Henry wanted to own every mine, forest, and rubber tree that went into the manufacture of his cars. Wood for floorboards and station-wagon panels came from here, but such operations were eliminated when grandson Henry II streamlined the company.

As the road comes down a long slope and passes the town of L'Anse, part of beautiful Keweenaw Bay spreads across your windshield. Scenic inlet of Lake Superior and bird sanctuary, this is a wonderful place to stop and focus on geese, ducks, red-winged blackbirds, or hawks—and now and then an eagle on the horizon. Visit the unusual statue of Baraga, heroic priest for whom the county was named.

Baraga's new historical museum on the bay has racks of data and Indian artwork, plus information on Las Vegas–style gambling in town, run by residents of the L'Anse Indian Reservation.

For back-roaders a choice detour from Baraga would be M-38 to Prickett Dam Road, then south toward Silver Mountain and the Sturgeon River Falls and Gorge. This "Grand Canyon of Michigan" is one of the deepest crevices in the Midwest.

In the town of Chassel (back on U.S. 41), old is in. There are antiques among the junk and junk among the antiques; for foraging searchers, a couple of good stops. The Strawberry Festival is the town's July gala.

We are on the threshold of Copper Country; little known, undersung; a territory America's legend preservers almost forgot. Unless you wear earmuffs and blinders, you will pick up parts of the story, but to travel here with no background would be like camping at Gettysburg without knowing there was a Civil War.

Five thousand years ago, Indians from another part of the continent came to Keweenaw Peninsula, dug copper out of shallow pits, and left. Eons later voyageurs found chunks of solid copper at surface level. In 1830 geologist (later governor) Douglass Houghton said the rumors of copper were true (rumors that it was thickly laced with silver were not true). Soon prospectors, gamblers, and investors (some backed by eastern wealth) took the hard road north, facing ice, hunger, and conniving competition to stake their claims; the prize was the purest copper ever found on Earth. Most of them died in poverty, but the overall take went beyond the richest days of the silver strike in Colorado or the gold rush in California.

Places named Dreamland, Hell, and Bootjack sprang up, with bawdy ladies and sly-eyed shysters, shanty towns and company towns with rows of identical roofs. Cornishmen,

Finns, Italians, Poles, and Croats poured in (or were recruited overseas) for mine jobs until the multiethnic population of Calumet grew to 47,000. Jenny Lind and Sarah Bernhardt appeared at the sumptuous Calumet opera house, the first municipally owned theater in America. The capital of the state was nearly moved to Keweenaw.

Every rip-roaring drama seen in Western mining movies has been lived on the Copper Country stage. Today the big payload is gone and most mines are sealed, but since 1845, 10 billion pounds of copper came up from 11,000 miles of deep underground tunnels. One mine shaft went down for more than a mile and a half.

This incredible era has not worked into our mythology the way Western stories did. Yet there is hardly a mile on U.S. 41 from this point on without traces of the fantastic events in Copper Country.

When U.S. 41 runs along Portage Lake, glimpses of a gray beach appear. The "beach" is stamp sand, dumped residue from an operation that crushes rock to release bits of copper. Endless tons of the gritty stuff make the lake and its inlets a lot smaller than nature intended. Not nice to walk on.

A sign of the pleasant present is that of the "Summer Place," one of the best restaurants in the U.P., a smallish cottage-turned-dining-room just before you reach Houghton. Reservations are recommended for their gourmet-level meals.

As Portage Lake narrows into a channel, the twin cities of Houghton and Hancock rise on identical mirror-image hills, as though they were on bleachers watching a parade. U.S. 41 passes through the campus of Michigan Technological University, a full-course school, outstanding for mining engineers. Their Seaman Mineral Museum is a course in itself.

Driving up and down the hilly streets of Houghton or Hancock in summer can be tricky enough; amid winter's icy coatings it smacks of San Francisco with a Norse devil in charge.

Northbound U.S. 41 travels the center of town (southbound takes another street), past vintage buildings of reddish
Jacobsville sandstone, another Keweenaw export that has
shown up in Chicago and New York. Note how parking
meters are backed against storefronts to avoid being buried by
snowplows. (Snow is thought of in feet instead of inches.) A
mine of gossip and current events is the Library Bar and Grill
near the dock of the *Ranger III*, the ferry to Isle Royale.*
Ramada, Best Western, fast food; not *too* quaint.

In crossing the bridge (an impressive hydraulic lift affair)
to Hancock, note the tidy small building on the right. It's the
oldest synagogue in this part of the state.

In Hancock, a tad smaller than Houghton, think Finland.
Home to Suomi College, the only place in the United States
where you can major in the Finnish language. Street names
are in Finnish and laundromat gossip between the grandmas is
bound to be in Finnish. The Finnish Heritage Center displays
the best of their arts, and has an auditorium and research facilities with living heritage tapes for anyone wanting to trace
their Helsinki connections.

The route winds uphill to a grand lookout point with a
graphic chart worth a thousand words.

Atop Hancock's hill, as much a symbol of the area as anything else, stands the Quincy No. 2 mine shaft house, all that's
left of an awesome operation. Down, down, *down* they went,
9,600 feet into the earth; men and tools to dig at hearts of
copper. That's the equivalent of seven stacked New York
World Trade Centers or six of Chicago's Sears Towers.

The elevator machinery that managed to tow men and
metal (no high-hazard pay in those days) up and down such a
distance can be seen during the summer months in a Steam

* Beautiful Isle Royale National Park would be a worthwhile destination for a
future country roads trip.

Hoist building next door. The long tilt of the shaft house roof shows the angle of entry into the earth.

For decades Quincy No. 2 stood dignified and rusting at the crest of the hill, a symbol of survival, stalwart aging subject of a thousand camera studies and paintings. However, folks who put beauty before character prettied it up with a bright new surface, and something wonderful is gone with the facelift. Had it rusted too far and become dangerous? It makes me sad.

"Hell," a boisterous saloon of a place, was on top of this hill, but all that's left are weeds and small gray houses. (There's another "Hell" in Livingston County on the Lower Peninsula.)

U.S. 41 rides through the center of Keweenaw, and we'll stick to that, but roads in any direction lead to scenery, history, and fun discoveries such as homemade ice cream or antiques at buyable prices. Totally uncrowded and lovely picnic places line the east shore.

Past the airport (with regularly scheduled flights), you can turn right into Laurium (hometown of football's "Gipper") or left into fabled Calumet, a shadow of its former self but no ghost town yet. In Calumet, they have recently restored the old opera house, which was built in 1900 at a cost of $70,000—back when that equaled millions.

You will note a high count of churches in Calumet (five visible from the same corner). At first, Italian Catholics declined to worship with Polish Catholics, and Latvian Lutherans couldn't understand Estonian Lutherans. Language differences and fierce pride were part of life when the city still had a hustle to it. The churches seem to have consolidated since.

Thurner's Bakery is a Calumet institution I recommend. You can also visit the Coppertown U.S.A. Museum on Red Jacket Road for more facts. Among copper souvenirs, only the nuggets are probably entirely local.

The "Hut" on U.S. 41 may have an unusually dim interior, but happily the cooks have good lights on what they're doing, and the food shines. Across the road is a stately Victorian home, the Garnet Bed & Breakfast. Built by a mining captain who loved bevelled glass and imported fireplaces, the spacious, gracious old place has had tender loving care and it shows.

Another popular eatery—best between this point and Copper Harbor—is the Country Cupboard in Kearsarge.

Kearsarge may be "The Last Place on Earth" according to Tom Manniko, who has given his shop this rather hopeless name. Tom also calls himself the Spoonmaker, and is really a cheerful sort who makes lustrous spoons and bowls out of local woods. His wife does pen-and-ink drawings of old houses, mine shafts, and the like with considerable skill. There are antiques and a few jams and candies to mull over while deciding between spoons or selecting a drawing to take home.

Copper City, Ameek, Allouez, Fulton, and others were all communities around mine locations—some still have the word "location" in their names.

Approaching Phoenix and Central (don't expect towns, just a few relics), meadows and second-growth trees stretch on one side of the road; the rugged heights of the Cliff Range on the other. A church at Central holds annual reunions where old-timers remember the hard days as though they were steady picnics. Cliffs pocked with mine probes are among the world's oldest rocks, once soaring higher than the Rockies.

The Delaware Mine offers an excellent tour and info and will tell you what to expect if you take the road to Bete Gris . . . aside from an isolated beach of singing sand and a small beauty of a bay.

U.S. 41 now dives into another of Michigan's tree-tunnels, an absolutely enchanting, rolling road under a shelter of northern hardwoods, birch, and pine. Sunlight filtering through the bright golds and reds of September makes it a fairy-tale lane, a dream world.

Watch carefully for the sign to Mandan and a dirt road that common sense might warn you about. However, unless there has been a week of heavy rain, go in for a short block, then park and hike. On a "street" roughly parallel to U.S. 41 are the empty windows and fallen porches of a real ghost town, not quite totally deserted. Several of the two-story houses have owners and part-time occupants; the others are too dangerously decayed to enter. But they are fun to look at and speculate over.

Mandan used to be the end of the line for a trolley coming up from Hancock and Calumet. Its citizens were all miners, of course, and the big weather-shocked house at the end of the block probably belonged to a boss.

The canopy of trees opens up as you approach Lake Medora, then closes in again. A low stone wall running through the brush on the right will indicate nearness to the Keweenaw Mountain Lodge, a small jewel among resorts. Probably the only county-owned and -operated facility of its kind in the nation, the lodge and nine-hole golf course were built during the Depression as a make-work project for unemployed miners. An immense fireplace dominates the dining room; there's another in the lounge, where the public or house guests can enjoy breakfast, lunch, or dinner next to windows on the woods or gardens. Duplex guest cabins all have fireplaces and modern baths, and the price is very right.

After the lodge (made entirely of local timber and full of windows) was completed, it was decided to add a basement. Great. You don't dig basements here, you blast them out. However, those miners knew exactly what they were doing and dynamited a large basement without taping or breaking one pane of glass upstairs.

A mile farther and you're in Copper Harbor, a one-time shipping point for copper and supplies and now a resort village right off a travel ad. Groceries, rock shops, boutiques, a museum, hearty meals by ladies who cook like mom, arts and crafts, motels, boats to rent, and a ferry to Isle Royale. It's hardly six blocks from one end of the hamlet to the other, and the population shrinks to a few dozen in winter. Just enough to keep a teacher hired for the one-room school.

The gentleman who runs the neat Brockway Motel is also the postmaster; the lady who owns the Country Store (the red and white farmhouse at the main intersection) is a leader of local tourism. Everybody does double duty as a guide, fish expert, historian, hunter, or rock hound.

If the water is calm, try to visit the lighthouse, now a small marine museum. On a point owned by private interests, the only way to legally get there is by boat at the west end of the harbor. Great for photographs of wave action against a rugged shore.

Down the road past the Fanny Hooe Resort are the Estivant Pines, a stand of tall virgin timber that miraculously escaped when everything was being cut down for mine bracing, railroad ties, and miners' housing. Among soaring venerable giants filtering the sunlight and giving voice to the wind, a long trail and a short trail wind their way in and out of hidden gullies and steep places; a world of lady ferns and bright mushrooms, trillium, and red/tart/juicy thimbleberries. The sharp-eyed may find traces of a village once sheltered by these trees.

A mile east of Copper Harbor, Fort Wilkins was built in the 1800s to guard copper miners from Indians, but was used mostly to guard the miners from each other. It is now the restored drawing card of a 200-acre state park between Lake Superior and Lake Fanny Hooe. The fort exhibits (including musket firings in summer) are exceptional, and you even get the feeling that military assignment here might not have been all bad.

One of the prehistoric mine pits is in the park, and a walking session with one of the park rangers is enlightening.

Beyond Fort Wilkins, the end of the road. U.S. 41 goes into a small loop and you are on your way back (to Florida?).

Not quite yet. Instead of returing to U.S. 41, take Brockway Mountain Drive (west side of Copper Harbor) for the most scenic drive in the state—and a whole "country roads" chapter of its own (see Chapter 17). The Drive climbs steeply at first, and you must take time to enjoy the lookout at the second bend. Copper Harbor lies below you, looking like a village under a Christmas tree as you can see the whole length of Lake Fanny Hooe to the hills beyond.

Take the other road down toward M-26 and Eagle Harbor, a beach hamlet inlet where the Knights of Pythias were founded. Maybe its time for a good supper at the Shoreline Restaurant in the village.

M-26 swings in and out along a rock-bound coast, past the agate-hunter's shores and high dunes of Great Sand Bay to Eagle River, Keweenaw County seat where the first courthouse in Michigan is still used.

Back to U.S. 41, following the siren call of side roads, poking through more towns. Check into a mansion on Tamarack Street in Laurium for a sumptuous bed-and-breakfast (tooled elephant hide on the dining room walls was installed by the 1903 owner). Off M-26 near Laurium, walk carefully to a slippery gorge and 120-foot Douglass Houghton Falls, highest in the state. The Arcadia Mine tour in Ripley near the Lift Bridge takes visitors into its rock world through an opening in the hillside—the *real* Copper Country.

Yet there's more. Silently waiting in the hidden glens of Keweenaw are old railbeds, dumped copper, botanical gems . . . whatever. Exploring U.S. 41's last northern lap can take a while.

For More Information

Ludington House Hotel, 906-786-4000

Fayette Historic State Park, 906-644-2603

Marquette County Tourism Council, 906-226-6591

National Ski Hall of Fame, 906-485-6323

Van Riper State Park, 906-339-4461

Michigamme Lodge, 800-358-0058 or 906-339-4400

L'Anse/Baraga Chamber of Commerce, 906-524-7444

Baraga Historical Museum, 906-353-8444

Library Bar and Grill, 906-482-6211

Best Western, 906-482-5000

Copper Country Chamber of Commerce, 906-482-2388

Finnish Heritage Center, 800-682-7604 or 906-482-5300

Quincy Mine Steam Hoist, 906-482-3101

Calumet Theater (Opera House), 906-337-2610

Coppertown U.S.A. Museum, 906-337-4354

Keweenaw Tourism Council, 906-337-4579

The Hut Restaurant, 906-337-1133

Garnet Bed & Breakfast, 906-337-5607

Country House Restaurant, 906-337-4626

Tom Manniko "Last Place on Earth," 906-337-1014

Delaware Mine, 906-286-4688

Keweenaw Mountain Lodge, 906-289-4403

Fanny Hooe Resort, 906-289-4451

Brockway Motel, 906-289-4588

Mariner North Restaurant, 906-289-4637

Harbor Haus, 906-289-4222

Fort Wilkins State Park, 906-289-4215

Shoreline Restaurant, 906-289-4637

Laurium Manor Inn Bed and Breakfast, 906-337-2549

19

Blue Sky, White Water, Black River

(CR-513)

Getting there: Take I-75 north to the Upper Peninsula and exit in Dafter. Take M-28 west through Munising and Marquette, and on to Bessemer, almost on the Wisconsin border. CR-513 turns north at Bessemer's only stoplight.

Or, take U.S. 41 and U.S. 141 north from Chicago through Wisconsin and into the Upper Peninsula. Join M-28 at Watton, Michigan, drive west to Bessemer, and go north on CR-513 at the Bessemer stoplight.

Highlights: See the seven waterfalls of the Black River; enjoy wildlife and fishing, Ottawa National Forest, an unusual ski jump, Black River Harbor, and Lake Superior.

Bessemer, the country-friendly seat of Gogebic County, lies nearly 600 miles from Detroit and about as far west in the state as you can travel. The population is not much over 2,500. Restock the picnic hamper and check camera supplies as you go through; running out of film on County Road 513 can be a major depressant.

North from Bessemer's only stoplight, CR-513 provides a 15-mile channel through the Ottawa National Forest. Behind mature hemlock and hardwoods east of the road, cutting a valley of its own design, the Black River bends, churns, and spills toward Lake Superior; a splashing ballet of seven waterfalls over roughly polished rocks to a smooth exit. The Black River heads Michigan's whitewater list, and this is the largest concentration of waterfalls in the state.

But wait. Before reaching most of the waterfalls, adventurers should examine a platform in the sky where humans have taken for themselves a space belonging to eagles.

The blacktop curves gently past aging trees and ancient stone chunks, outcroppings of the precambrian shield, some of the oldest exposed rocks on earth. Huge black crows gather around roadside carrion and reluctantly take flight when a car passes. By August, wood ferns are knee-high. Now and then a black bear might saunter across the road in early dawn or a snowy owl will soar overhead. Thimbleberries (very tart and red, raspberry-shaped with wide leaves) are not uncommon if you wander into the trees.

About nine miles along CR-513 and a mile down Copper Peak Road waits the parking lot and gift shop/ticket office of Copper Peak Ski Flying Hill (elevation about 1,500 feet above sea level). The western hemisphere's tallest ski jump perches upon this shoulder of rock, high ground for championship ski flying competitions. In summer anyone who can manage height and the low price of a ticket can go up to the top.

Part A in getting up there is a chairlift ride over the jagged side of the peak. Eight hundred feet up on a cliff edge, the ski jump, only partially visible before, comes into full and scary view. Feeble jokes pass between visitors mustering the courage to go on. Is this a playground slide for King Kong?

The slide support tower encloses a 20-story elevator ride (Part B of the venture) to a concrete platform with chain-link walls up to the ceiling (formed by another platform overhead). The spot would make an alpine goat feel at home. Beautiful. A lot of people (perhaps a majority) have no wish to go farther. However, climbing the final 60 feet to the very top of the slide (Part C) is the only way to get a true ski flyer's-eye view staring down the chute—down, down, down to a hopelessly tiny patch of earth that has shriveled to Kleenex-size since you were at ground level.

The 80-plus steps to the ultimate top are not on the slide itself, and feel quite solid. Railings are high and tight. Forget that this part is cantilevered out into space. The very slight sway is normal for any steel structure this high (240 feet). Without flexibility the tower could snap.

When there are no more steps to climb and you can look about, the moment pounds at your senses. The view down the chute grabs you and won't let go.

Imagine winter and a huge crowd of expectant faces far below. Snow. Gray skies, colorful clothes. Banners, judging stands, press boxes. Persons who have spent their lives practicing to be birds check their skis one more time, then drop down that one-way alley into sheer space, landing (usually) in one piece. The best ones "fly" 500 feet or more.

For non-skiers, the slide view can only be handled in small doses. Better to turn toward Lake Superior and the misty shores of Minnesota or to western horizons in Wisconsin. The Black River really *looks* black from up here; the forest ripples with a dozen shades of green.

Back at the base, mugs, badges, and postcard reminders can be purchased. Yet clearly, the mind able to forget Copper Peak is beyond nudging.

Only a few miles to a Michigan waterfall extravaganza. The first with parking and a trail is Great Conglomerate Falls,

named for those masses of pebbles and
gravel cemented into larger rocks ("pud-
ding stone").

The forest rings with eerie quiet till
bird calls and a rush of wind open
new valves in your head. Slowly,
steadily, soft sounds are lost in the rising crescendo of falling
water. Down a gnarled natural staircase formed by networks
of tree roots and you meet the source of the roar head-on. A
tumbling caldron in springtime, still pouring prettily in
autumn, Great Conglomerate and its gorge are as beautiful as
a promise kept.

Around a big chunk of rock, down into the canyon, water
races between boulders and bubbles over itself. On higher
banks tall pines lean toward the action.

Less than a mile farther along CR-513, a large parking
loop lets pilgrims choose among five falls including Potawatomi Falls and Gorge Falls. These two are connected by a trail
lovely enough to win a place on the National Recreational
Trails roster.

Wide platforms allow for different views of the cascades
and river; benches and perching spots give more time to let
the swift flow rinse out the musty corners of one's soul. (How
can you question platforms and stairs, built to protect people
from treacherous slopes and to guard slopes from damaging
overuse? These wooden aids are handsomely made and
needed, but still seem an intrusion on a pristine setting.)

The gorge at Potawatomi is around 30 feet deep, and geol-
ogists can point out traces of an ancient lava flow or tilted
thrusts of mountains worn down to shadows of the past.
Gray-streaked boulders and water-buffed ledges squinted at
from across the stream melt into abstract artworks.

Viewing Gorge Falls involves tackling a long flight of steps,
but there are plenty of bench stops. The river narrows, then
plunges through a smooth steep-walled slot with great drama.
One sticklike trunk in a rock crevice is all that's left of a brave

tree once trying to grow on the cliff face where water volume in spring would drown anything.

Another jewel in the chain, Sandstone Falls, can be enjoyed with little hazard from river level after a steep climb. Time now to take off shoes and dangle feet in the rushing water, a cool massaging sensation, or (in drier seasons) to sit on a slab in midstream.

The softer nature of sandstone has made this viewer-friendly spot vulnerable to the turning currents. Water has scooped dozens of bowls and half-bowls out of the rocks as if it were a frenzied potter.

Climbing down to Rainbow Falls is made easy by a long flight of steps that seems to go on forever. The thought that what goes down must go up may tempt the timid to quit midway, but at this beauty spot the water takes the longest leap of all—40 feet—and it shouldn't be missed. A sign tells of danger on slippery rocks, probably one of the most ignored warnings around, even though the views from the safer platforms are excellent.

The Black River has now dropped about 1,000 vertical feet in its serpentine path from its source in Wisconsin 30 miles away. There are other falls (without parking lots and groomed paths) and a hiking trail connects all that have been mentioned here. Although it's not a walkway for once-a-year hikers, the adrenaline induced by the beauty of the river is enough to send anyone into training.

At road's end, the adventure changes gear. Black River Harbor is not a wide-open bay, but an intimate outlet to Lake Superior. Two rocky breakwaters spread their arms to form a Harbor of Refuge, one of the safety inlets that have been built about every 30 miles along the Great Lakes. Boats bob on their moorings near picnic tables, and about 40 campsites are available to those pulling trailers; others for tents are nearby.

Across a rustic suspension bridge and through the woods (watch for more thimbleberries) to the waiting beach where a grand broad vista of open lake awaits. After surviving a trek

to Copper Peak and hikes to five waterfalls, a feeling of playing Walter "Balboa" Mitty finally reaching the Pacific can be
overwhelming. . . . Congratulate yourself with a restorative
R&R period at water's edge.

For More Information

Gogebic Area Visitors and Convention Bureau, 906-932-4850

Ironwood Tourism Council, 906-932-1122

Upper Peninsula Travel and Recreation Association,
906-774-5480

Index